DAD JOKES

THE PRICELESS EDITION

First published in Great Britain in
2022 by Cassell, an imprint of
Octopus Publishing Group Ltd
Carmelite House
50 Victoria Embankment
London EC4Y 0DZ
www.octopusbooks.co.uk

An Hachette UK Company
www.hachette.co.uk

Distributed in the US by
Hachette Book Group
1290 Avenue of the Americas
4th and 5th Floors, New York,
NY 10104

Distributed in Canada by
Canadian Manda Group
664 Annette St., Toronto,
Ontario, Canada M6S 2C8

ISBN 978 1 78840 258 3

A CIP catalogue record for
this book is available from the
British Library.

Printed and bound in the UK

10 9 8 7 6 5

Publisher: Stephanie Jackson
Editorial Assistant: Louisa Johnson
Designer: The Oak Studio
Art Director: Jaz Bahra
Production Controller: Serena Savini

This FSC® label means that
materials used for this product
have been responsibly sourced.

MIX
Paper from
responsible sources
FSC® C104740

DAD ✳
JOKES
THE PRICELESS
EDITION ✳

Kit & Andrew Chilvers

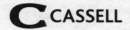

Dedicated to our old mate Andy Delaney (Sand), who has never opened one of these books and has no idea we're dedicating this to him.

Introduction

Blimey, here we are again! So, here's another annual compendium of gags to keep those guffaws going deep into next year. And we thought this dad joke malarkey was just a brief flash in the pan.

As always, we'd like to shout out to our brilliantly droll, witty community of japesters on Twitter, Instagram and Facebook, who are always there with hilarious caption ripostes that are often funnier than the original jokes.

Once again, let's just have a laugh and make our world a funnier, sunnier place.

Lots of love,

Kit & Andrew

I told my son he shouldn't
listen to losers.

Now he won't talk to me.

———————

What has three letters and
starts with gas?

A car.

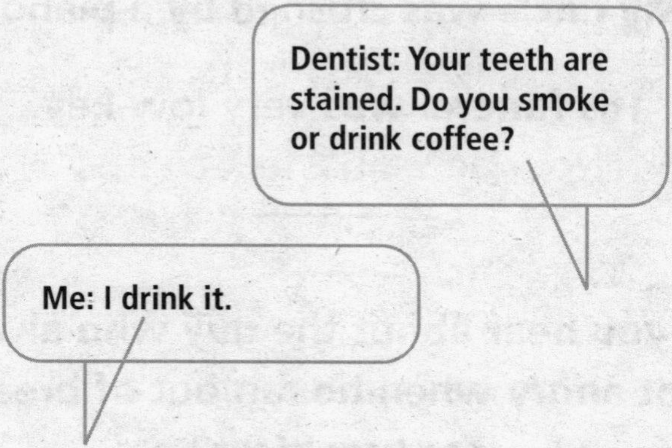
Dentist: Your teeth are stained. Do you smoke or drink coffee?
Me: I drink it.

My uncle was crushed by a piano.

His funeral was very low-key.

―――――

Did you hear about the guy who always got angry when he ran out of bread for breakfast?

He was lack-toast intolerant.

What's the difference between
a camera and a foot?

A camera has photos, while a foot
has five toes. . .

_____

My girlfriend says I'm way too
condescending.

(That means I speak down to people.)

A history degree is useless.

There's just no future in it.

Why did the coward suddenly feel brave after touching a rock?

Because he felt a little boulder.

———————

I can't believe someone broke into my house and stole all of my fruit.

I am peachless.

Our local auctioneer has passed away.

He was somewhere around
30? 35? 35? 40!

_____

There's this new cryptocurrency
called Decibel.

It's a sound investment.

I have a friend who really hates living in the centre of the USA.

She says she's in a constant state of Missouri.

————————

Did you hear about the giant with diarrhoea?

It's all over town.

Why do wood carvings take so long?

Because they have to be done whittle by whittle.

My co-worker Celsius needed to take some time off, so they hired a guy called Kelvin to cover for him.

He's the new temp.

What do you call someone who's really good at darts?

Amy.

_____

What dating app do lumberjacks use?

Timber.

I have a fear of overly intricate buildings. . .

I suppose you could say I have a complex complex complex.

———————

What do the French call it when something sad happens on Thursday?

Un tra-jeudi.

My cloning experiment's finally paid off!

I'm so excited, I'm beside myself.

Why does Spider-Man's calendar only have 11 months?

He lost May.

———————

I watched a documentary on how ships are kept together.

Riveting.

The Earth's surface is 70 per cent water.
That water is uncarbonated.

Therefore, the Earth is flat.

_____

My wife left me because I couldn't
stop doing impressions of pasta.

Now I'm cannelloni.

I said to the customer, "So, you'd like a cheeseburger?"

"Yes," he said. "Well done"

"Thank you," I said.

———————

I just flew back from a *Transformers* convention.

And boy, my arms are tyres.

Tomorrow, my son and I are getting new glasses. And after that?

We'll see.

My wife says the salads I make tend to be a bit on the "dry" side.

It's definitely something that needs addressing.

———

I'm not a competitive person. . .

. . . I'll be the first to admit it.

Bros don't let other bros walk around with an open fly.

It's called the zip code.

―――――――――

Which actor does the least driving?

Christopher Walken.

Boss: Thanks for filling in the job application form. Do you have any experience?

Me: Yes. This is my 20th interview.

Two trees got arrested in my town yesterday.

I heard they've been up to some shady business.

———————

My wife dated a clown before she started going out with me.

It's fair to say I had some pretty big shoes to fill.

What's the scariest kind of plant?

BamBOO!

———————

I just finished reading a great book about an immortal cat.

It was impossible to put down.

Me: Hello, I'd like an oxtail please.

Butcher: Certainly. Once upon a time, there was an ox. . .

My wife said to me, "You really have no sense of direction, do you?"

"Whoa," I said. "Where did that come from?"

———————

I tried to come up with a carpentry pun that woodwork.

I think I nailed it, but nobody saw.

What did Elton John say when he saw a pet rabbit at the gym?

"It's a little fit bunny. . ."

———————

Sad news, my giant parrot died today.

Mind you, it's a huge weight off my shoulders.

Teslas do not have that
"new car" smell. . .

They have an Elon Musk.

———————

Vin Diesel eats two meals a day:

breakfast and breakfurious.

Taxi driver: Do you mind if I put some music on?

Me: Not at all.

Taxi driver: Kiss?

Me: Hmm, let's listen to the music first and see how we feel.

A genie granted me one wish, so I said, "I just want to be happy."

Now I'm living in a cottage with six other dwarves and working in a mine.

What do you get if you put a duck in a cement mixer?

Quacks in the pavement.

I gave my friend an apple, but he told me he preferred pears.

So I gave him another apple.

———

It hurts me to say this. . .

. . . but I have a sore throat.

My wife and I always argue over the right way to hang the toilet paper roll, so our therapist suggested we each try it the other person's way for a week.

You know – roll reversal.

———

What's the difference between a literalist and a kleptomaniac?

A literalist takes things literally. A kleptomaniac takes things, literally.

I'm trying to learn the alphabet, but I can't get past X.

I don't know why.

_____

If you ever find yourself becoming demotivated, try drinking a gallon of water before going to sleep.

That'll give you a reason to get out of bed in the morning.

Interviewer: How do you explain this four-year gap on your résumé?

Me: Oh, that's when I went to Yale.

Interviewer: That's impressive. You're hired.

Me: Thanks. I really need this yob.

Why did Novak Djokovic pay for his flight to Australia with a Mastercard?

Because his Visa didn't work.

———————

My wife told me, "I can think of 14 reasons to leave you, plus your obsession with tennis."

I replied, "That's 15, love."

My balloon elephant wouldn't fit
on the back seat of the car.

So I had to pop the trunk.

————————

My son's fourth birthday was today,
but when he came to see me, I didn't
recognize him at first.

It was as if I'd never seen him be four.

Insomnia is terrible.

But on the plus side. . . Only three more sleeps until Christmas.

———

What crime do blacksmiths most commonly get charged with?

Forgery.

My friend has
designed an
invisible aeroplane.

I can't see it
taking off.

How would a proud computer dad introduce his son?

A microchip off the old block.

———————

I've started a flight company exclusively for bald people.

It's called Receding Airlines.

I found a coin on the street the other day, and it had teeth marks all over it.

It was a Bitcoin.

———

When I was a kid, I wanted to play the guitar really badly.

And after years of hard work, practice and dedication, I can now play the guitar – really badly.

My boss always laughed at my jokes in the office, but since we started working from home, she never laughs at them in our Zoom chats. I asked her why.

She replied, "Because your jokes aren't remotely funny."

_____

Why are the great pyramids in Egypt?

Because they were too heavy to carry off to the British Museum.

I asked my dad how it feels to have the best son in the world.

He told me to ask my grandpa.

————————

I came home drunk last night, and my wife said, "How much have you had to drink?"

"Nothing," I slurred.

"Look at me!" she shouted. "It's either me or the pub – which one is it?"

I paused for a second to think, and then mumbled, "It's you. I can tell by the voice."

Me: I'm sorry I'm late, boss. I was having computer problems.

Boss: Hard drive?

Me: No, the commute was OK. It's my laptop.

Which kind of fish is made out of two sodium atoms?

Two Na.

_____

I never remember what people tell me at New Year's Eve parties.

It just goes in one year and out the other.

It doesn't matter whether you're the
Queen of England or a school kid.
At the end of the day. . .

. . . it's night.

————————

My wife asked me why I want to
be cremated.

I told her it's because it's my last chance
to get a smoking-hot body.

If you're unable to hold your bladder
in the Netherlands. . .

. . . European.

_____

Have you heard about the political
party that's using really good weed to
promote their opinions and agenda?

It's propaganja.

I've just invented the first thought-controlled air freshener.

It makes scents when you think about it.

My wizard friend asked me to proofread one of his scrolls the other day.

Well, it was more of a spellcheck, actually.

I had a debate with a Flat Earther once. He stormed off in a huff, saying he'd walk to the edge of the Earth to prove me wrong.

I'm sure he'll come around, eventually.

My wife just called me pretentious.

I was so surprised, my monocle fell out.

Does anybody know where a guy can find a person to hang out with, talk to and enjoy spending time with?

Asking for a friend.

How can anyone think the Academy Awards are real?

I watched it, and it's obvious that everyone there is a paid actor!

You know what they say about cold spaghetti.

Those who forget the pasta are doomed to reheat it.

Dad: Look, just stop it.

Me: Why?

Dad: Don't do that. You always question my authority.

Me: How?

I went to McDonald's and ordered two large fries.

They gave me about 75 tiny ones instead.

———

For a practical joke, I came into the office early this morning and switched the "m" and "n" keys on as many keyboards as I could. Some might call me a monster, but. . .

. . . the rest are goimg to call ne a nomster.

I was having some computer issues, and the IT guy said I had to clear my cache of cookies.

I've done as he said, but I don't see how eating 300 Oreos is going to make my laptop work better.

_____

How do gamers like to shower?

With Steam.

Why do the numbers three and five make such a great team?

Because together, they thrive.

———————

Before we were married, my partner used to clean up my place, and I used to clean his.

Eventually, we realized we were maid for each other.

Did you hear about the pole vault champion of North Korea?

He's now the pole vault champion of South Korea.

———

What's the difference between a tapeworm and the Eiffel Tower?

One's a parasite, and the other's a Paris site.

It's been months since I placed my order for a copy of the book *How to Scam People Online*.

It still hasn't arrived.

———————

My wife said she'll divorce me if I keep making puns about birds with long necks.

That's swan way to go about it.

I saw a squirrel that just couldn't make up his mind today.

He was on the fence all day.

———

Did you hear about the town that legalized weed but banned alcohol?

The residents were left high and dry.

I picked up a hitchhiker last night. He asked, "How do you know I'm not a serial killer?"

I replied, "The chances of two serial killers being in one car are astronomical."

———————

Why are archaeologists so good at romance?

Because they have the best dating techniques.

My friend just sent me a strange text message. It said: "There's a man on the bus next to me who keeps farting."

"It could be worse," I replied. "At least he isn't on your bus."

———————

What's the difference between a cranky two-year-old and a duckling?

One is a whiny toddler, and the other is a tiny waddler.

If slow old people use walking sticks, what do fast old people use?

Hurry canes.

———————

When I was just a little kid, I used to pray for a bicycle, but my Sunday school teacher told me that's not how prayer works. So I stole a bike. . .

. . . and prayed for forgiveness.

I've been trying to understand why
my candle can't sleep.

I guess there's just no rest for
the wicked.

Why is your nose in the middle
of your face?

Because it's the scenter.

If Apple made a car, what would be missing?

Windows.

_____

Where do couples go to argue when they're at the mall?

The feud court.

A B-flat, an E-flat and a G-flat walk into a bar.

The bartender says, "Sorry, I don't serve minors."

If you're ever locked out of your house, start talking to your lock, calmly and clearly.

After all, good communication is the key.

_____

What do you call nitrogen that just finished eating?

Nitrate.

**What's the best way to watch
a fly-fishing tournament?**

Live stream.

———————

How do two arsonists hook up?

A match on Tinder.

Did you hear about the guy who broke the world record for fitting into the largest shoes?

It was no small feet.

Why are rotten eggs like dads?

They both have bad yolks.

Tesla founder Elon Musk is originally from South Africa, which is strange.

I always thought he was from Mad-at-gas-car.

_____

I told my friend that my New Year's resolution is to do yoga every morning.

"Sounds like a bit of a stretch," he replied.

As I looked at my naked body
in the mirror. . .

. . . I realized that I was going to
get kicked out of IKEA.

———————

I got my Covid test result today.
It says 50 – what does that mean?

Also, my IQ test came back positive.

Genie: OK, I'm going to grant you one wish. What do you wish for?

Me: I wish I could be you.

Genue: Weurd wush, but U wull grant ut.

My dad always told me I should marry an ancient Egyptian.

He said they make great mummies.

———————

What's the difference between black-eyed peas and chickpeas?

Black-eyed peas can sing us a song; chickpeas can only hummus one.

My yoga instructor
was drunk today.

Put me in a very
awkward position.

What do you call a sugar and marzipan Christmas cake that isn't yours?

Stolen.

Why do clumsy farmers make good DJs?

They're always dropping the beets.

**What do you call a snake
without any clothes on?**

S-naked.

_____

**What happens to an illegally
parked frog?**

It gets toad.

Which country is filled with
bodybuilders?

Liftuania.

_____

I met Tom Hanks once. He was so rude!

I asked for his autograph, and all he
wrote was "Thanks".

Me: Even though you've been married to grandma for 50 years, you're still so romantic. You still call her "darling", "honey", "love" . . . What's the secret?

Grandpa: I forgot her name ten years ago, and I'm scared to ask her.

What's the difference between a sweet potato fresh out of the oven and a pig thrown off a balcony?

One is a heated yam and the other is a yeeted ham.

I put my phone under my pillow last night. When I woke up, it was gone and there was a $1 coin in its place.

It must have been the Bluetooth Fairy!

What did the atheist beaver say
when he died and went to hell?

"Well, I'll be dammed."

_____

What word in the English language
is always spelled incorrectly?

Incorrectly.

I need help.
Someone glued
my deck of cards
together.

I don't know how
to deal with it.

My girlfriend and I were kissing on the sofa, and she said, "Let's take this upstairs."

"OK," I said. "You grab one end, and I'll grab the other."

———————

According to a recent survey, heterosexual men say the first thing they notice about a woman is her eyes.

Women say the first thing they notice about men is that they're a bunch of liars.

What do you call Batman after he's had his ass kicked in a fight?

Bruised Wayne.

_____

What do you call someone who handles the finances of an ant colony?

An account-ant.

I asked my wife why we never talk about gravity.

She said it just never seems to come up.

———————

I dressed up as a screwdriver at Halloween.

It wasn't the best costume, but I still turned a lot of heads.

There's a reason Daniel Craig has greying hair in the latest Bond movie.

He had *No Time To Dye*.

Did you hear about the ATM that got addicted to money?

It suffered from withdrawals.

On rainy days, my wife thinks it's pathetic when I stare through the window.

It would be less pathetic if she just let me in.

————————

Did you know that plateaus. . .

. . . are the highest form of flattery?

What's the worst thing to say before a driving test?

"This thing does have airbags, right?"

———————

Today was the first time I made money as a computer programmer.

I sold my laptop.

I recently applied for a job as a spy.

They told me to send in my résumé and undercover letter.

A shark can swim faster than me, but I can run faster than a shark. . .

So in a triathlon, it would all come down to who is the better cyclist.

Last night, I went out for dinner with a boxer.

She went for the ribs.

———————

Thieves have stolen 20 crates of Red Bull from my local shop.

I don't know how these people sleep at night.

My wife gave birth in our car on the way to the hospital.

I named him Carson.

What's a cat's favourite pistol?

A Meowser.

———————

My boyfriend borrowed $100 from me. After three years, when we separated, he returned exactly $100.

I lost interest in that relationship.

A photon checks into a hotel.

"Do you have any luggage?"
the receptionist asks.

"No," says the photon.
"I'm travelling light."

_____

How many bones are in a hand?

A handful.

What's a forklift?

Food, usually.

———————

Yesterday, I went to a DIY place to get manure for my garden. They were out of stock, so I complained.

I wasn't taking sh*t from anyone that day.

I'm writing a book about reverse psychology.

Please don't buy it. . .

————————

I told my girlfriend I think she's cheating on me.

She told me I sound just like her husband.

How many country singers does it take to change a light bulb?

Two: one to change it, and one to sing about how much they miss the old one.

An infinite number of mathematicians enter a bar. The first orders a pint of beer. The second orders half a pint, the third a quarter, ad infinitum.

The bartender just pours two pints and says, "Figure it out yourselves."

I've created a word-processing
programme to rival Microsoft.

It's their Word against mine.

———————

Why is it cheaper to throw a party
in a haunted house?

Because the ghosts will bring the boos.

My grandpa was in a band called The Hinges.

They once opened for The Doors.

_____

What do you call an incompetent hangman?

The bearer of bad noose.

I've just applied for a job in a salad-packing factory.

The hours are terrible, but apparently the celery is good.

Where do vampires get their pencils?

Pennsylvania.

———————

All of my friends have such
impressive bucket lists.

Mine is a little pail in comparison.

If Tesla made a gun, what would it be called?

Elon Musk-et.

———————

I saw two gentlemen on the street arguing over a bus pass.

It was a fare fight.

My uncle has two Dobermanns
named Rolex and Timex.

They're watchdogs.

_____

What's the difference between
a pirate and a cranberry farmer?

One buries his treasure, and the
other treasures his berries!

What happened when the comedian started telling twice as many dad jokes?

His audience doubled in sighs.

What's small, red and whispers?

A hoarse radish.

Can someone please tell me what the lowest rank in the army is?

I've been trying to find out for ages, but every time I ask someone, they tell me, "It's private."

————————

I told my cat that I'm going to teach him to speak English.

He looked at me and said, "Me? How?"

Did you guys hear about the underwear thief?

The police said it was a brief case.

Our computers went down at work today, so we had to do everything manually.

It took me 20 minutes to shuffle the cards for Solitaire.

Furniture salesperson: This sofa is really spacious – it can seat five people without any problems.

Me: Where the hell am I going to find five people without any problems?

Why are there Pop-Tarts,
but no Mom-Tarts?

Because of the pastry-archy.

_____

Jokes about sugar are rare.
Jokes about brown sugar?

Demerara.

I found a 55-inch TV on Craigslist for only £20 because the volume was stuck on full.

Wow, I thought to myself. *I can't turn that down.*

**The first floor is going great,
but the second floor. . .**

. . . Well, that's another storey.

**What's big and white
and can't climb trees?**

A fridge.

I'll be sharing my secret for being an amazing guitar player later today.

Stay tuned.

Why doesn't Bruce Banner tear his trousers when he becomes the Hulk?

Because the radiation altered his jeans.

I heard Arnold Schwarzenegger was just hired to star in a new film about classical composers.

He'll be Bach.

_____

In Germany, they even have a sausage made out of other sausages.

It's the wurst of the wurst.

What do you call a hotel breakfast that gives you diarrhoea?

Incontinental.

———————

What does garlic do when it gets too hot?

It takes off its cloves.

What did one monocle say to the other?

"Let's get together and make a spectacle of ourselves."

———————

Once upon a time, there lived a king who was exactly 30 centimetres tall.

He was a terrible king, but he made a great ruler.

What crime was the fussy baby charged with?

Resisting a breast.

_____

I've been trying to find a precise definition for the word "ambiguous".

It's unclear, inexact and open to more than one interpretation.

Why did the Spider-Man in the alternate universe do better on his driver's test?

Because, naturally, he's a parallel Parker.

————————

What do you call a boat full of buddies?

A friendship.

Apparently, 30 per cent of pet owners let their pet sleep in their bed.

I tried it, and my goldfish died.

Flight attendant:
Hello, there, sir.
Would you care for
an orange juice?

Me: Sure, if it needed
me to.

God initially intended to use wasps to pollinate flowers.

But in the end, He went with plan bee.

———————

I asked my partner when his birthday was. He said, "March 1st."

So I walked around the room and asked again.

What do two chefs do after they get married?

They consommé the marriage.

_____

What is a lawyer's favourite drink?

Subpoena colada.

A policeman spotted an elderly lady knitting while driving.

"Hey," he said. "Pull over!"

"No," she replied. "It's a scarf!"

———————

I'm getting a reversible jacket for Christmas.

I can't wait to see how it turns out.

I haven't sold a single copy
of my autobiography.

It's just the story of my life.

———————

What's the difference between
a dog and a well-dressed man?

The man wears a perfectly tailored
three-piece suit. The dog? Just pants.

What do you call a murderer who has recently exfoliated?

A smooth criminal.

Why do they say "be there,
or be square"?

Because you're not a-round.

_____

I got fired from the keyboard
factory today.

They said I wasn't putting
in enough shifts.

I had an excellent meal last night at this cosy little Christian restaurant near us called The Lord Giveth.

They also do takeaways.

_____

What breed of roosters lays eggs?

Himalayan.

How do you hide a vintage video game before Christmas?

You put the cartridge in a pear tree.

———

I called the tinnitus helpline. . .

. . . but it just kept ringing.

Great house cleaners are not born. . .

. . . they're maid.

**What do they serve for breakfast
in earthquake zones?**

Panquakes.

What do you call the man who shreds your cheese at a restaurant?

Not sure, but he seems like a grate guy.

**Did you hear the Incredible Hulk
has started recycling?**

He's really going green.

**I saw my son eating chocolate, even
after I had confiscated all his Halloween
candy. I asked him where he got it from.**

**He said, "I always have a few Twix
up my sleeve."**

What's a thousand times better
than Instagram?

Instakilogram.

My girlfriend treats me like a god.

She ignores my existence and only talks
to me when she needs something.

I told the waiter my steak was bad.

He picked it up, slapped it and threw it back down, then said, "If it gives you any more trouble, just let me know."

———

What kind of fruit do ghosts like?

Boo berries.

Did you hear about the criminal who was aroused by semantics?

He got off on a technicality.

What do laxatives and seat cushions have in common?

They're both stool softeners.

———

Which body part is most reliable?

Well, you can always count on your fingers.

I heard you can get lawyers at IKEA now.

They're very affordable, but you have to build your own case.

———

I recently came into a lot of money. . .

. . . and that's why I got fired from the bank.

What do they call the employee
of the month at the crematorium?

The top urner.

———————

My wife left me for another man.
All that lies ahead now is a miserable,
pointless, lonely life.

And while he's going through that,
I'll be down the pub with my mates
every night.

What do you call a Swedish telemarketer?

A Scamdinavian.

_____

My next-door neighbour just knocked on my door with her dinner in her hands.

It turns out Facebook and Instagram are down, and she just wanted me to see what she was eating.

Sarcasm doesn't get you anywhere.

Well, it got me to the Sarcasm World Championships in Mexico '98.

Really?

No. . .

What kind of horses come out after the sun sets?

Nightmares.

_____

I had the rudest, slowest, nastiest cashier today!

I guess it's my own fault for using the self-checkout lane.

A ghost who used to haunt me as
a kid visited me again last night.

Gave me déjà BOO!

———————

What do you call a fish without an eye?

Fsh.

Where do you find a crab with no legs?

Exactly where you left it.

Penguins produce an oil that helps their feathers retain heat.

So it's true what they say:
the oily bird gets the warm.

———————

I heard that you should always look into a mirror before making a big decision.

It helps you reflect.

I took all my savings out of the bank
and put the cash on a boat.

I feel much better now that my money
is offshore.

———

Why do fishermen do well at geometry?

They are good anglers!

If you're a comedian, never do
a show for ghosts.

There's a 100 per cent chance
you'll get booed off the stage.

———————

I'm writing a book about all the things
I should be doing with my life.

It's an oughta-biography.

Have you heard about the big dental convention they're holding in Nevada?

It's called Floss Vegas.

———————

I've just invented a machine that can create facsimiles of prosthetic appendages.

Essentially, it's a faux-toe-copier.

I used to read comic books,
but I stopped.

They're just far too graphic.

———————

With great power comes. . .

. . . a great electricity bill.

I just broke up with my mathematician girlfriend.

She was still obsessed with her x.

———

I once dated a magazine collector.

Let's just say he had issues.

I threw a ball for my dog.

It's a bit extravagant, I know, but it was his birthday – and he looks great in a tuxedo.

To whoever stole my cow:

my beef is with you, sir!

———————

Sadly, the guy who invented the fruit smoothie has passed away.

He's being berried on Friday.

Why didn't the skeleton cross the road?

Because he had no stomach for it.

I loaned my grandfather clock to my friend and he still hasn't returned it.

He owes me big time.

_____

That guy stole my place in the queue.

I'm after him now.

When you're waiting for the waiter. . .

. . . you *become* the waiter.

Where do bicycles go for a drink around here?

Handle bars.

What do a tight pair of underpants and a small terraced house have in common?

No ballroom.

What do you call a bloodsucking tax specialist?

Account Dracula.

Do you know any good corn jokes?

I'm all ears.

———————

What do you call an anti-vax nanny?

Mrs Doubt Pfizer.

I went to see a psychic, but she was in a bad mood. Then I tried a clairvoyant, but he was really grumpy.

I'm just trying to find a happy medium.

We started a band and called it Books.

We're hoping it means no one will judge us by our covers.

———————

You shouldn't eat more than
239 beans in one sitting.

One more would be too farty!

I was going to tell a joke about
sodium and oxygen. . .

. . . but I'm afraid I'd get a violent
reaction.

———————

My brother just started dating
a girl called Rosemary.

I don't know what he season her.

I recently befriended a ghost who keeps wheezing all the time.

I named him Gasper.

———————

A mate of mine just got a smart washing machine that's Wi-Fi enabled.

I told him not to let it on social media, or it'll air all his dirty laundry.

What do you call an ancient Greek who is just a bit, well, average?

Mediocrates.

I saw a bunch of batteries gathered around in a circle.

I guess they were having an AA meeting.

———————

What do cars spread on their toast?

Traffic jam.

My wife left me
because I didn't
do enough chores
around the house.

I'm devastated. . .
I didn't do much
to deserve it.

How did the phone propose to his girlfriend?

He gave her a ring.

———————

What's the term for when a person dies and comes back as a hillbilly?

Reintarnation.

What did Arnold Schwarzenegger say when his wife asked him why he hadn't updated to Windows 10?

"I still love Vista, baby!"

_____

My friend stole one of my board games, so I took one of theirs for revenge.

They took a *Risk*, but now they don't have a *Clue*.

My son asked me why I was washing the dishes while sitting down.

I told him it's because I can't stand doing it.

———————

Did you know that bees are actually allergic to pollen?

It makes them break out in hives.

I started my own all-natural fertilizer company recently.

I guess that makes me an entre-manure!

———————

Why do computer programmers prefer to work the dark?

Because the light attracts bugs.

What car does a Jedi drive?

A Toyoda.

**What do you call a Grim Reaper
with hearing problems?**

Deaf.

What did the judge say to the dentist?

"Do you swear to pull the tooth, the whole tooth and nothing but the tooth?"

_____

What do you call a one-legged hippo?

A hoppo.

Robber: Give me all your money, or you’re geography!

Bank manager: Wait, what? Don’t you mean history?

Robber: Don’t change the subject!

Why did the Cyclops stop teaching
at the school?

Because he only had one pupil.

———————

Why don't pirates like travelling
on mountain roads?

'Scurvy.

Who's the genius that decided to call it "emotional baggage" and not "grief case"?

My partner just broke up with me. He says my life revolves around football, and he's sick of it. I'm quite upset.

We were together for seven seasons.

_____

My dad was down at the auto dealership, looking at potential choices. Examining one of the vehicles, he asked, "Hmm. . . cargo space?"

The salesperson said, "Um. Car no do that. Car go road."

Where do maths teachers go on vacation?

Times Square.

_____

I'd like to have kids one day. . .

I don't think I could stand them any longer than that, though.

I'm opening a chain of Elvis-themed steak restaurants. . .

They'll be for people who love meat tender.

Where do wolves like to stay while on vacation?

At the Howl-iday Inn.

Apparently, to start a zoo you need at least two pandas, a grizzly and three polars.

It's the bear minimum.

———————

What's the opposite of Antarctica?

Uncle Arctica.

I mistakenly took a ten-minute video of my shoes yesterday.

It was an accident, but I actually got some pretty good footage.

I'm thinking of removing my spine.

I think it's the only thing holding me back.

_____

The CEO of IKEA was just elected Prime Minister of Sweden.

The first thing he'll need to do is to assemble his cabinet.

Kid: Dad, do trees poop?

Dad: Where do you think number two pencils come from?

I asked my dog, "What's two minus two?"

He said nothing.

_____

Tablets were replaced by scrolls, then scrolls were replaced by books. . .

. . . and now we scroll through books on tablets.

For her birthday, I took my wife to an orchard, and we stood there looking at the trees for half an hour.

Apparently, it was not the kind of Apple Watch she was expecting.

———————

Why was the moon detained?

Lunacy.

My therapist told me to write letters to everyone who's hurt me, then burn them.

I've done that, but what do I do with the letters?

———————

My wife threatened to leave me if I didn't stop making *Star Wars* puns.

I guess divorce is strong with this one. . .

My six-year-old is the only one in his class who doesn't believe in Santa.

He's a rebel without a Claus.

_____

Fun fact: oxygen solidifies at -218.79°C.

That's *really* cool.

When my dad was unemployed, he used to hide money in the bushes in our garden.

He went on to become a successful hedge-fund manager.

My wife said if I bought her one more stupid gift, she would burn it.

So I bought her a candle.

I just got a job in a factory making plastic Draculas.

There are only two of us working on the production line, so I have to make every second count.

**What has two grey legs
and two brown legs?**

An elephant with diarrhoea.

**How do two French guys share
files electronically?**

They use a Pierre-to-Pierre network.

Did you hear about the mechanic
who fell asleep under the car?

He woke up oily in the morning.

A man walks into the doctor's office
with a frog on his head.

The doctor says, "Can I help you?"

"Yes please," says the frog. "Can you cut
this wart off my rear end?"

Who hides in the bathroom at parties?

The party-pooper.

_____

What do you call a sexy flying monkey?

A hot air baboon.

Waiter: All finished, sir? How did you find your steak?

Dad: I just looked next to the potatoes, and there it was.

My inflatable house got a puncture last night.

Now I'm living in a flat.

Why should you never brush your teeth with your left hand?

Because a toothbrush works better.

I returned my lizard to the pet store
because he wouldn't stop telling
dad jokes.

"That's not a lizard," the shop assistant
told me. "That's a stand-up chameleon."

———————

15 + 15 = 30.

16 + 16 = 30 too.

Who were the greenest Presidents in US history?

The Bushes.

David Beckham gets in a taxi and realizes the driver is staring at him in the rear-view mirror.

After two minutes without moving, the driver says, "Go on, then. Give me a clue."

Beckham replies, "OK, I played for Manchester United and England and married a Spice Girl – is that enough?"

"No, David," says the driver. "I meant where are you going?"

———————

Why didn't Hans Solo enjoy his steak dinner?

It was Chewie.

I tried flushing my Dutch slippers
down the toilet.

Now the drain is all clogged up.

_____

What do you call the sexuality where
you're attracted to both men and
women, but neither is attracted
to you?

Bi-yourself.

I had a broken neck last year,
which wasn't much fun.

But at least now I can look back
and laugh.

———————

If you think swimming with dolphins
is expensive, you should try swimming
with sharks.

It cost me an arm and a leg!

**What did the shipmates find
in the toilet?**

The captain's log.

———————

What do you call sweaty boobs?

Humidititties.

I've got a condition that causes me to make terrible puns.

It's a dad-ly disease.

———————

I went to a bookstore and saw a book called *How to Solve 50 Per Cent of Your Problems*. I bought two copies.

What did the
surgeon say to
the patient who
insisted on closing
his own incision?

"Suture self."

What's the difference between
a bowl of mouldy lettuce and
a depressing song?

One is a bad salad, and the other
is a sad ballad.

———————

I was going to propose to my girlfriend,
but my dog ate the ring.

Now it's a diamond in the ruff.

Why do librarians hate tennis?

Too much racket.

———————

The other day, my wife asked me how
I became so damn good at making love.

I told her she should thank all the
women who came before her.

Daughter: Dad, what's your password?

Dad: MickeyMinnie GoofyDonaldPlutoHuey LouieDeweyDublin.

Daughter: Wow, why's it so long?

Dad: Because they said it had to contain at least eight characters and at least one capital.

You should always fear a pirate duck.

He has the power to unleash
the quackin.

———————

I tried to bring my oversized board
game on to the plane with me, but
I wasn't allowed.

They said the Risk was just too big.

What do you call a castrated unicorn?

A eunuchorn.

_____

That's the tenth passenger today who's called me a terrible bus driver.

I don't know where these people get off.

What tastes better than it smells?

A tongue!

————————

My girlfriend complains that I don't smile anymore.

Well, she's the one who wanted a serious relationship!

Archaeologists are holding a party to celebrate unearthing the largest ever dinosaur tibia.

It's going to be quite the shindig.

When I was young, my mum used to tear out the last page of all my comics. She wouldn't tell me why.

I had to draw my own conclusions.

———————

A boy asked his Bitcoin-investing dad for one Bitcoin for his birthday.

His dad said, "What? $15,554? $14,354 is a lot of money! What do you need $16,782 for, anyway?"

Which Disney princess spends most of her day on dating apps?

Tinderella.

What's the difference between a cat and a frog?

A cat has nine lives, but the frog croaks every night.

At the weekend, I like to play chess with elderly men in the park.

But it's becoming increasingly difficult to find exactly 32 of them.

———————

My wife and I were really happy for 20 years.

Then we met.

What's the most desired summer body
this year?

The antibody.

_____

Two sausages are sizzling away in a pan.

The first one says, "Oh, man, it's hot
in here!"

The second one says, "AHHHH!!!
A TALKING SAUSAGE!!!"

What do you call a kangaroo wearing a sweater?

A woolly jumper.

_____

My next-door neighbour and I were very good friends, so we decided to share our water supply. . .

. . . because we got along well.

I have the attention
of a goldfish.

Seriously, it's been
watching me
for hours.

What did you get your son for his birthday?

I got him an alarm clock that swears at him instead of beeping.

Wow, sounds like he's in for a rude awakening.

Which insect is high in cholesterol?

A butterfly.

_____

I don't understand all this controversy around cloning.

Clones are people two.

My grandfather was terrible until I had my first child.

Now he's a great-grandfather.

———————

I grilled a chicken for two hours.

It still wouldn't tell me why it crossed the road.

I was all set to become one of the world's greatest mountain climbers. . .

. . . but I peaked too early.

———————

My last girlfriend said I was unnecessarily mysterious.

Or did she?

I couldn't sleep last night,
so I read a dictionary.

By 3am, I was past caring.

_____

One of my daughters wants
to marry the postman. . .

. . . but I won't letter!

Farmers are leaving Facebook in their droves.

Every time they put down a post, somebody takes a fence.

———————

What flavour is the toothpaste in jail?

Imprisonmint.

My friend once used laughing gas as deodorant.

He smelled funny the whole day.

———————

My mate broke his leg, so I wrote "You are stupid" on his cast.

I was just adding insult to injury.

Pandora's box wasn't actually a box.

In fact, all that trouble started because it was ajar.

How long is one minute?

It depends what side of the bathroom door you're on.

I once dated a condemned witch.

There was a lot at stake in the relationship, but now she's just an old flame.

———————

My friend Tony asked me not to say his name backwards.

I asked, "Y not?"

Why did the mystic refuse Novocaine?

He wanted to transcend dental medication.

Doctor: How have you been since our last appointment? Have you managed to reduce the cigarettes you smoke?

Me: Oh, yes. They're definitely shorter by the time I've finished them.

My mum is a radiologist. She met my dad when he came in for an X-ray.

I wonder what she saw in him.

_____

I'm trying to organize a hide-and-seek tournament.

But good players are really hard to find.

What do you get when you mix a penis, a potato and a boat?

A dick-tator-ship.

————————

Someone called me lazy today.

I almost replied. . .

After I went to the dentist, I headed to the studio and recorded a gospel album. My mouth was still numb, so I was drooling the whole time.

The album's called *Songs of Salivation*.

———————

Did you hear the semicolon got arrested?

It got two back-to-back sentences.

A lot of people can't tell the difference between entomology and etymology.

I can't find the words for how much this bugs me.

———

My psychiatrist says I have an unhealthy obsession with revenge.

We'll see about that. . .

A man is told that his local bank is currently offering mortgages with no interest. He heads along to the branch to find out more.

"Hello," he says. "I'm here to enquire about your mortgages."

The bank manager replies, "I don't really care."

What's worse than raining cats and dogs?

Hailing taxis.

Me: Hi, can I borrow *Batman Forever*?

Video-store manager: No, you'll have to bring it back tomorrow.

I've decided to name my son Mark.

That way, when I die, I'll be able to say I left a Mark on this world.

———————

What did the farmer say when all of his haystacks were stolen?

"This is the last straw!"

I really wanted to become a monk.

But I never got the chants.

My doctor has advised me to stop drinking. It's clearly time for me to make a massive change.

It's going to be tough; I've been with that doctor for 15 years.

———————

What do you call a knight who loves to scare people?

Sir Prise.

I always take my problems to Tommy.

Hilfiger something out.

———————

Why do cow-milking stools only have three legs?

Because the cow has the udder.

Therapist: What brings you in today?

Me: I have a terrible fear of tsunamis.

Therapist: How bad is it?

Me: It comes in waves.

Does anyone know any good sword-fighting puns?

I'm trying to think of any words that have a duel meaning.

After staying silent for a long time, I finally told my hot co-worker how I felt.

They felt the same way.

So, I turned on the air conditioner.

I'm a fisherman, and I'm dating
a mermaid.

I met her online.

———

I quit my job as a scuba-diving instructor
after giving my first lesson.

Deep down, I knew it wasn't for me.

I finally finished childproofing my home, but I didn't do a very good job.

My kids are still able to get into the house.

I'm in a band called Dyslexia.

We've just released our compilation album, *Greatest sHit*.

———————

I told my son to go and find out what *"nada"* means in English.

He came back with nothing.

A door-to-door salesperson knocks on the front door of a house.

It's answered by a 12-year-old, holding a glass of cognac and smoking a cigar.

The salesperson asks, "Are your parents home?"

The kid replies, "What do you think?"

———

When Bill and Melinda Gates got divorced. . .

. . . Melinda got the house, but Bill kept the Windows.

Breaking news: historians believe that they've uncovered a cache of pencils that once belonged to William Shakespeare.

A spokesperson said, "They're so badly chewed on the ends, we can't tell if they're 2B or not 2B."

My friends love scaring the crap out of me.

With friends like that, who needs enemas?

Doctor: How's your broken arm feeling?

Me: Pretty sore.

Doctor: Do you think painkillers will help?

Me: It wouldn't hurt.

My friend was bragging that his new 3D printer can print a gun.

Big deal. I've had a Canon printer for years.

Once again, I've entered our town's annual Tightest Hat Competition.

This year, I'm really hoping I can pull it off.

What's the worst thing about having a job at the unemployment office?

If you get fired, you still have to show up the next day.

I went to an Indian restaurant and asked for some garlic bread.

But they had naan.

I'm having a hell of a time getting this yoga instructor to leave my house.

Every time I ask her to leave, she just says, "Namaste."

———————

What do you call a cruise ship filled with skilled artisans?

Great Craftsman Ship.

Why isn't 24 July a holiday?

Are we really expected to work 24/7?

———————

How do you make antifreeze?

You take away her blanket.

I saw a deer on the way to work this morning.

How do you know it was on its way to work?

I've trained my dog to go and fetch me a bottle of wine.

He's a Bordeaux collie.

———

Never scream into a colander.

You'll strain your voice.

My teacher asked me to make up a sentence using the words "defence", "defeat" and "detail".

I wrote: "When a horse jumps over defence, defeat go first, then detail."

Our doorbell rang and my son called to me, "Dad, there's a salesperson here with a moustache!"

I yelled back, "Tell him I've already got one!"

My wife asked if I think our kids are spoiled.

"No," I said. "I think most kids smell that way!"

Just had a police officer at the door saying he was looking for a man with one eye.

I told him to use both: he'd probably find him a lot quicker that way.

———————————

I asked my dad why he decided to buy a boat.

He said, "There was a sail."

I gave my daughter a watch for
her birthday.

When she showed it to the next-door
neighbour, he said, "That's a pretty
new watch you've got there!
Does it tell you the time?"

She laughed and said, "No, this is
an old-fashioned watch! You have
to look at it."

_____

Why do people wear shamrocks on
St Patrick's Day?

Real rocks are too heavy.

What's the highest rank in the popcorn army?

Kernel.

_____

A platypus walks into a bar owned by a duck.

The platypus finishes his drink and asks to pay.

Duck billed platypus.

What do you call a walking mosquito?

An itch-hiker.

What does a clam do on his birthday?

He shell-ebrates.

If H20 is on the inside of a fire hydrant, what's on the outside?

K9P.

_____

I got fired from Uber.

Apparently, they didn't like it when I went the extra mile.

Why is the letter "a" like a flower?

Because a "b" comes after it!

———

What is the smelliest kind of ox?

A buttocks.

My wife accused me of hating her family.

"That's not true," I told her. "Your mother-in-law is way better than mine!"

What happens when you put your hand in a blender?

You get a handshake.

———————

What is a doctor who specializes in Adam's apples called?

A guyneckologist.

What type of haircut does
Steven Spielberg get?

The director's cut.

———————

I recently joined a support group
for people who talk a lot.

We call ourselves On and On Anon.

Hey, Dad, what does déjà vu mean?

I have a feeling you've asked me this before.

Since Facebook claims ownership of everything you post on their website. . .

. . . I've decided to start uploading my electricity bills.

I decided to stop walking under billboards after one collapsed on top of me.

I took it as a sign from above.

What did the movie director say before shooting a dangerous stunt scene?

"It's a take I'm willing to risk."

———————

My girlfriend left me while I was crying in the bathroom with constipation.

She told me that I was so full of it.

It was the hardest dump I ever took.

How many wives can a monk have?

Nun.

I finally found a genie in a bottle!

I asked him if it would be possible to change French positives to Spanish.

He replied, "*Oui* shall *sí*."

_____

What do you call someone who can't stop watching films with strong female leads?

A heroine addict.

How did the computer eat its supper?

In megabytes.

_____

Which bones drive other bones to work?

The metacarpools.

I looked out of the window and was surprised to see my dad slumped over the lawnmower, crying his eyes out.

I asked my mum, "What's up with him?"

"Oh," she said. "He's just going through a rough patch."

—————————

What do you call a polar bear in the jungle?

Lost.

What do you call a horny square?

An erectangle.

I asked my German friend if he knew the square root of 81.

He said, "*Nein.*"

We only bought this bottle of wine yesterday. Why is it half empty?

Maybe it's because you're a pessimist.

There are four quarters in
the Superbowl.

And that's why they brought out
50 Cent at half-time.

———————

What are the two steps to marrying
a country girl?

First: a tractor.

Next: fertilizer.

Someone complimented me on my driving the other day. They left a note on my windshield.

It said: "Parking fine".

───────────

Why do nurses always carry a red pen with them?

In case they need to draw blood.

Why did doctors name them haemorrhoids?

Asteroids was taken.

———————

What do you call a sleepy relative?

Nap-kin.

I met a ventriloquist at a bar who told me I was attractive.

I wasn't sure if it was her or the beer talking.

What is as big as a hippopotamus but weighs nothing at all?

A hippopotamus's shadow.

————————

What do you call a crocodile that loves guacamole?

A guacodile.

I slept like a baby last night.

I woke up every two hours and cried.

_____

My partner threatened to leave
me because of my obsession
with optical illusions.

I said, "Wait! This isn't what
you think it is!"

My mum told me to go the shop.
She said, "Get one carton of milk
and if they have avocados, get six."

When I got back, she looked at
what I'd bought.

"Why did you buy six cartons of milk?"
she asked.

I replied, "Because they had avocados."

What is muffins spelled backwards?

Exactly what you do when you take
them out the oven.

How much do dumplings weigh?

Wonton.

_____

Why did the baker's wife divorce him?

Because he was too kneady.

@DadSaysJokes is a community-run dad jokes network on Instagram, Facebook and Twitter, with over 5 million collective followers, inspired by the daily jokes of author Kit Chilvers' dad, Andrew.

Every day, followers submit their jokes and the team picks their favourites – or Dad just drops in his own zinger!

Kit, a young social networking influencer, started his career at the tender age of 14, when he created his original platform, Football.Newz. He has since added another fourteen platforms, including @PubityPets and monster meme Instagram page @Pubity, which has over 31 million followers.

Also available:

 @DadSaysJokes

 @Dadsaysjokes

 @DadSaysJokes

AROMATHERAPY

IN A NUTSHELL

AROMATHERAPY
A STEP-BY-STEP
GUIDE

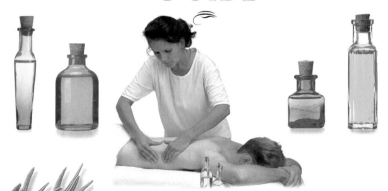

SHEILA LAVERY

mustard

First published in
Great Britain in 1997 by
ELEMENT BOOKS
LIMITED Shaftesbury,
Dorset, SP7 9BP

This edition is published and
distributed by Mustard

This edition published 1999
Mustard is an imprint of Parragon

Parragon
Queen Street House
4 Queen Street
Bath BA1 1HE

NOTE FROM THE PUBLISHER
Any information given in this book is
not intended to be taken as a replacement
for medical advice. Any person with
a condition requiring medical attention
should consult a qualified practitioner
or therapist.

Designed and created with
The Bridgewater Book Company Ltd

ELEMENT BOOKS LIMITED
Managing Editor Miranda Spicer
Senior Commissioning Editor Caro Ness
Group Production Director Clare Armstrong
THE BRIDGEWATER BOOK
COMPANY LTD

Art Director Peter Bridgewater
Designers Andrew Milne,
Jane Lanaway
Page layout Chris Lanaway,
Sue Rose
Managing Editor Anne Townley
Picture Research Lynda Marshall
Three dimensional models Mark Jamieson
Photography Ian Parsons, Guy Ryecart
Illustrations Andrew Milne, Andrew Kulman
Text consultants BOOK CREATION SERVICES LTD
Series Editor Karen Sullivan

Printed and bound in Portugal

British Library Cataloguing in
Publication data available

Library of Congress Cataloging
in Publication data available

ISBN 1–84164–254–1

The publishers wish to thank the
following for the use of pictures: A–Z
Botanical Collection Ltd: pp.22TR,
34TL, 36TL, 38TR, 42TL, 44TL,
50TL; Bridgeman Art Library:
pp.8TL, 8/9; e.t.archive: p.9T; Harry
Smith Collection: pp.30TL, 32TR, 40TL,
46TL, 48TL; Image Bank: pp.11BR, 52B

Special thanks go to:
Tom Aitken, Cheryl Butler, Carly Evans, Julia
Holden, Simon Holden, Stephen Sparshatt
for help with photography

Ken Gross. The Plinth Company Ltd,
Stowmarket, Suffolk
for help with properties

Contents

What is aromatherapy?

THE TERM AROMATHERAPY *is used to describe a particular branch of herbal medicine. It is coined from two words, "aroma" meaning pleasant scent and "therapy" meaning a treatment that aims to cure a physical or mental condition. Literally it means treatment using scents. The scents involved are not perfumes but the pure essential oils of plants valued for their therapeutic properties. Treatment involves applying these oils to the body to improve physical, mental, and emotional health.*

ABOVE **Flowers, leaves, herbs, bark, and roots are the five main sources of essential oils.**

LAVENDER

Essential oils are the basic tools of aromatherapy. The oils, which are extracted from plants (*see page 20*), can be used to treat all systems of the body, disturbances of the mind, and imbalances of the emotions. There are many ways to use essential oils. Professional aromatherapists tend to favor massage as the most effective way of getting oils into

ABOVE **For massage essential oils are diluted in vegetable oil.**

the body. Massage also increases the healing potential of aromatherapy. The medicinal properties of the oils and the nurturing power of touch combine to form a potent healing treatment. Massage can be relaxing or energizing, it can

SANDALWOOD

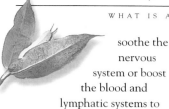

EUCALYPTUS LEAF

soothe the nervous system or boost the blood and lymphatic systems to improve physical and mental functioning.

Not least among its benefits is the way it can ease pain and tension from tense or overworked muscles and lift the spirits. Whenever possible, try to include massage in your home aromatherapy treatments; where this is not possible, use any of the other methods mentioned below and described in greater detail on pages 16–19.

ABOVE *Always warm massage oil in your hands before applying to the skin.*

RIGHT *Where a full body massage is not possible, a soothing back massage is often the next best choice of treatment.*

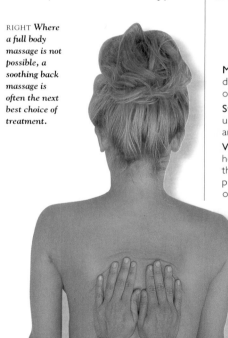

WAYS TO USE ESSENTIAL OILS

Massage using diluted essential oils.

Steam inhalations using essential oil and hot water.

Vaporizers use heat to release the scent and properties of the oils into the air.

Baths scented with the oils.

Compresses using pieces of cotton soaked in water and essential oils.

Creams, lotions shampoos and shower gels that have essential oils added to them.

Gargles and mouthwashes

Neat Some essential oils can be applied undiluted to the skin.

A short history

MOST ANCIENT CULTURES *valued the therapeutic benefits of aromatic plant oils. The ancient Vedic literature of India and historic Chinese medical texts document the importance of scented oils in promoting health and spirituality. Hippocrates, regarded as the "father of medicine," used fragrant fumigations to rid Athens of plague, and Roman soldiers were strengthened by scented oil baths and regular massage. But the richest aromatic traditions belong to the ancient Egyptians. Physicians from all over the world are reputed to have traveled to Egypt to learn aromatic medicine from these masters.*

ABOVE **Ancient Egyptians used fragrant oils such as cedarwood, frankincense, and myrrh in the embalming process.**

WESTERN DEVELOPMENTS

Aromatherapy is believed to have come to the Western world at the time of the Crusades. There are records of essential oils being used during the plague in the fourteenth century. But it was during the sixteenth and seventeenth centuries that aromatherapy was most popular. The great European herbalists, including the Englishman, Nicholas Culpeper, wrote avidly about its benefits. During the last two centuries scientists developed a greater under-standing of plant oil chemistry.

LAVENDER

BELOW **Four-thousand-year-old papyrus manuscripts record how the Egyptians used aromatic oils for religious and medicinal purposes.**

MODERN PIONEERS

Ironically, scientific research led to the growth of the drug industry and the demise of plant medicine. Then, in the 1920s, a French chemist, René Maurice Gattefossé, became intrigued by the healing potential of essential oils. He discovered that lavender oil quickly healed a burn on his hand and that many essential oils were better antiseptics than their synthetic counterparts. It was Gattefossé who coined the term *aromathérapie*.

ABOVE *Culpeper listed the properties of many herbs.*

Dr. Jean Valnet

A French army surgeon Dr. Jean Valnet furthered research by using essential oils to treat soldiers wounded in battle. Later he used the oils with great success on patients in a psychiatric hospital. In 1964 Valnet published *Aromathérapie*, which is widely regarded as the bible of aromatherapy.

Marguerite Maury

In the 1950s Madame Marguerite Maury, a beauty therapist, introduced aromatherapy clinics to Britain. She taught beauty therapists how to use essential oils in massage to provide a treatment which was suited to each individual client.

In recent years aromatherapy has developed far beyond beauty therapy. It is now a recognized and important part of complementary healthcare.

BELOW *Coriander has been used therapeutically for at least 4,000 years.*

How does aromatherapy work?

ESSENTIAL OILS *enter the body by inhalation and by absorption through the pores of the skin. They affect the system in three ways: pharmacologically, physiologically, and psychologically, as annotated below.*

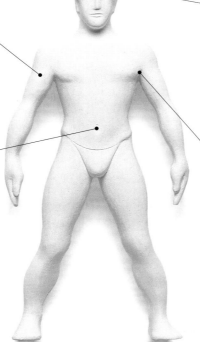

Once inhaled, aromatic signals are sent to the limbic system of the brain where they exert a direct effect on the mind and emotions

The chemical constituents of the oils are carried in the bloodstream to all areas of the body, where they react with body chemistry in a way similar to drugs

After several hours the oils leave the body. Most are exhaled, others are eliminated in urine, feces, and perspiration

Certain oils also have an affinity with particular areas of the body and their properties have a balancing, sedating, or stimulating effect on body systems

LEFT **It can take between 20 minutes and several hours for oils to be absorbed into the body, but on average it takes about 90 minutes.**

HOW DOES IT FEEL?

Depending on the choice of oils and method of treatment, aromatherapy produces any number of sensations. For most people safe treatment is pleasant, enjoyable, and relaxing.

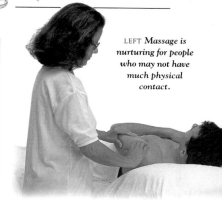

LEFT *Massage is nurturing for people who may not have much physical contact.*

LEFT *Lotions or masks containing essential oils are soothing for mild skin conditions.*

WHO BENEFITS?

People of all ages and levels of health can benefit. It is nurturing for babies and children and it gives many elderly people a feeling of being cared for. Pregnant women and even seriously ill patients can benefit from professional treatment.

WHAT DOES IT TREAT?

Aromatherapy benefits the person rather than their illness. But it has been shown to be particularly good for stress-related problems, muscular and rheumatic pains, digestive disorders, menstrual and menopausal complaints, anxiety, insomnia, and depression.

BELOW *A therapeutic bath is the easiest way to treat yourself at home.*

Oils are inhaled and absorbed

11

Treatment

THIS BOOK *is intended as an introductory guide and as a handbook for self-treatment. Aromatherapy is one of the most enjoyable of all complementary therapies and it is safe and easy to use at home, providing you follow certain basic guidelines.*

LEFT *Diluted oils can be applied locally at the site of infection.*

WHEN TO SEE A PROFESSIONAL

Always seek professional treatment for chronic or serious health problems or if a problem becomes severe or persistent. There are certain conditions for which self-treatment is ill-advised.

TREATING YOURSELF

Self-treatment is suitable for minor or short-term problems only. For example:

- Minor cuts, burns, and bruises
- Colds, flu, and chest infections
- Mild eczema, dermatitis, rashes, or stings
- Occasional bouts of constipation and diarrhea, hemorrhoids, and indigestion

- Occasional cystitis, painful or irregular periods, and mild PMS
- Short-term anxiety, tension, mild depression, and insomnia
- The conditions listed on pages 53–8

How many sessions are necessary?

The number of treatments required depends on the nature of the problem, the length of time you have had it, and how fast you heal. For relaxation, have as many treatments as you like.

Can I combine treatment with other therapies?.

Aromatherapy is compatible with conventional medicine and most other forms of holistic treatment. However, if you are taking medication, it would be wise to consult your doctor and your aromatherapist. Some essential oils are not compatible with homeopathic treatment.

WARNING

Consult a qualified practitioner for advice and treatment:

- If you are pregnant
- Have an allergy
- Have a chronic medical condition such as high blood pressure or epilepsy
- Are receiving medical or psychiatric treatment
- Are taking homeopathic remedies
- When treating babies or very young children

How to find a good quality oil

Choose only those bottles that are labeled "pure essential oil," which are undiluted and unadulterated. If in doubt contact one of the major aromatherapy bodies for a list of approved oil retailers.

ABOVE *Essential oils add a fresh, natural fragrance to lotions and potpourri.*

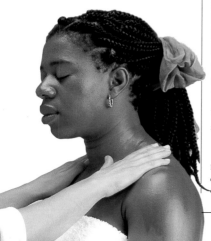

LEFT *If you want to use aromatherapy during pregnancy, it is wise to consult a practitioner.*

ROSEMARY

BLENDING OILS

Essential oils can be used alone or blended together. Oils are blended for two reasons: to enhance or change their medicinal actions and to create a more sophisticated fragrance. In perfumery many oils are blended together. For therapeutic purposes it is unusual to mix more than four oils together. When blending oils at home it is best to mix no more than two or three oils. This is because blending has been shown to alter the molecular structure of essential oils and you may end up with a blend that acts differently from what you had intended. Make sure the properties of the oils are complementary.

YLANG YLANG

BLENDING OILS FOR MASSAGE

1 Choose a light vegetable base oil such as grapeseed, sweet almond, or sunflower oil.

2 Add your chosen oils a little at a time, shake the bottle, and rub a little into the back of your hand to test. Adjust the quantities until you achieve the blend you want.

3 Mix in about five percent wheat germ oil to preserve the blend.

BLENDING GUIDELINES

Choose two or three oils which you believe complement each other. In general, oils from the same groups (citrus, floral, spicy, etc.) and those which share similar constituents blend well. Using the proportions detailed in the Techniques section, mix a blend using a little of the strongest scented oils and more of the lighter fragrances.

Throughout this book there are recipes for suggested blends. But be guided by your own likes and dislikes. The best blend is usually the one you find most appealing.

ABOVE *Oils may be extracted from different parts of each plant and blended with other oils to make an individual perfume or remedy.*

BELOW *Once blended, oils may be added to different bases, such as bubble bath, or stored in dark colored bottles.*

CAUTIONS
People with sensitive skin should introduce the oil with caution. NB: Myrrh should not be used during pregnancy. Do not swallow mouthwashes or gargles.

Aromatherapy techniques

THERE ARE MANY *ways to use essential oils at home. Massage and bathing tend to be the most popular and techniques which involve applying oils to the body are usually more effective than inhalation. However there are several other techniques which are particularly beneficial for certain conditions.*

ABOVE *Assemble everything you need for your treatment before you begin.*

BELOW *Use both hands to "mold" the body.*

MASSAGE

Dilute the essential oil in a vegetable carrier oil. Use 5 drops of essential oil to 1 teaspoon of carrier oil for adults, half that strength for children under seven and a quarter of the strength for children under three. Do not use essential oils to massage newborn babies.

BENEFITS: The most relaxing, luxurious, and therapeutic of all aromatherapy treatments.

DISADVANTAGES: You need to have a willing and able partner. Not suitable as a "quick fix."

BASIC MASSAGE TECHNIQUES

1 **EFFLEURAGE** *Place your hands flat on the bottom of your partner's back. Slide them upward, leaning into the palms to add pressure. At the shoulders, fan your hands out to each side and stroke lightly down each side. Repeat, varying the length of each stroke.*

2 **CIRCLING** *Place both hands on your partner, a few inches apart, and stroke in a wide circular movement. Press into the upward stroke and glide back down. Your arms will cross as you make the circle, so just lift one hand over the other to continue.*

3 **KNEADING** *Place both hands on the area to be massaged with your fingers pointing away from you. Press into the body with the palm of one hand, pick up the flesh between your thumb and fingers, and press it toward the resting hand. Release and repeat with the other hand.*

4 *Finish with gentle soothing strokes and end the massage by holding your partner's feet for a few seconds. Holding the feet helps to "ground" the person being massaged and brings them back to reality.*

STEAM INHALATIONS

• Add 3–4 drops of oil to a bowl of boiling water. Bend over the bowl, cover your head with a towel, and breathe deeply for a few minutes. You can also use this method as a facial sauna.

• **Benefits**: Quick and easy, heat increases the benefits of anti-infective oils.

• **Disadvantages**: Not always suitable for asthmatics; dangerous for children.

VAPORIZERS

• Can be electric or a ceramic ring that is heated by a light bulb, but most are ceramic pots warmed by a small candle. Add water and 6–8 drops of oil to the vaporizer. Alternatively, add the oil to a bowl of water and place by a radiator.

• **Benefits**: Scents and purifies the air, clears germs. Good for emotional and breathing problems.

• **Disadvantages**: One of the least effective ways to get oils into the body.

BATHING WITH OILS

For adults add 5–10 drops of essential oil to a full bath. Use less than 4 drops for children over two, and 1 drop for babies. Stir through the water with your hand. For footbaths use 2–3 drops of oil.

BENEFITS: Easy to use; relaxing.

DISADVANTAGES: None.

CREAMS, LOTIONS, AND SHAMPOOS

Add 1–2 drops of essential oil to creams, lotions, and shampoos and massage into the skin or scalp. Choose unscented products made from good quality natural ingredients.

BENEFITS: Convenient for everyday use.

DISADVANTAGES: May irritate sensitive skins.

ABOVE *Adding the oil to running water releases the fragrance.*
RIGHT *Steam inhalations work best for congestion, catarrh, and headaches.*

GARGLES AND MOUTHWASHES

Dilute 4–5 drops of essential oil in a teaspoon of brandy. Mix into a glass of warm water and swish around the mouth or use as a gargle. Do not swallow.

BENEFITS: Ideal for throat infections and mouth ulcers.

DISADVANTAGES: Not suitable for children; unpleasant taste.

WARNING

Never take essential oils by mouth. If swallowed accidentally, eat bread, drink plenty of milk, and seek professional help.

HOT AND COLD COMPRESSES

Add 4–5 drops of essential oil to a bowl of hot or cold water. Soak a folded clean cotton cloth in the water, wring it out, and apply over the affected area. If using a hot compress, cover with a warm towel and repeat when it cools.

• Hot compresses are good for muscle pain, arthritis, rheumatism, toothache, earache, boils, and abscesses.

• Cold compresses are good for headaches, sprains, and swelling.

Use a clean cotton cloth

Hold in place until pain eases

RIGHT **Hot and cold compresses can be used for pain relief.**

USING NEAT

A few essential oils such as lavender, tea tree, and sandalwood can be applied undiluted to the skin. Most oils should not be used neat as they can cause irritation.

Essential oils

ESSENTIAL OILS *are extracted from the leaves, flowers, fruit, wood, bark, and roots of plants and trees. They are natural multifaceted chemical compounds, more complex and safer than pharmaceutical drugs, but slower acting so they are best used as a preventive or as a complementary form of treatment.*

ABOVE *The oils are distilled soon after harvesting as plant material deteriorates rapidly.*

About 150 essential oils have been extracted for use in aromatherapy. Over the next few pages you will find detailed information about 15 of the most useful oils, all of which you can buy from specialist suppliers, healthfood stores, and some large pharmacies.

Each essential oil has a unique fragrance and at least 100 chemical components, which work together to heal mind and body. All the oils are antiseptic, and may have numerous other actions such as being anti-inflammatory, pain-relieving, or antidepressant. Every oil also has a dominant characteristic and is classified accordingly as stimulating, relaxing, or refreshing, for example. A few oils such as lavender are adaptogenic, meaning they do what the body requires of them at the time. Nobody really understands how essential oils affect body functioning in this way.

BELOW *Essential oils dissolve in oil or pure alcohol, but not in water.*

ABOVE *Essential oils should be stored out of children's reach and used within three months.*

HOW THE OILS ARE EXTRACTED

Most pure essential oils are extracted by a process of steam distillation, but other methods such as solvent extraction, enfleurage, and expression are also used. For optimum benefits, essential oils must be extracted from natural raw ingredients and remain as pure as possible.

YOUR 15 OILS

The oils on the following pages have been chosen for their safety, availability, price, and versatility. The blends are made from 10 drops of essential oil; adjust the quantities to suit your choice of technique. Occasionally, additional oils are mentioned in the remedies.

KEY TO DIFFERENT TECHNIQUES

The following symbols are used on pages 23–51.

 Massage

 Footbath

 Bath

 Inhalation

 Shower

 Compress

 Vaporizer

 Gargle

 Neat

 Shampoo

 Cream or lotion

 Mouthwash

 Damp cotton wool or dressing

Lavender

LAVANDULA ANGUSTIFOLIA

OF THE SEVERAL *varieties of lavender used medicinally,* Lavandula angustifolia *is the most important. It is the most versatile, best loved, and most widely therapeutic of all essential oils. Both flowers and leaves are highly aromatic but only the flowers are used to make essential oil.*

ABOVE *Lavender is a unique oil because it is so versatile; and it blends well with other oils.*

BELOW **The fragrant purple flowers are used to produce pale yellow oil.**

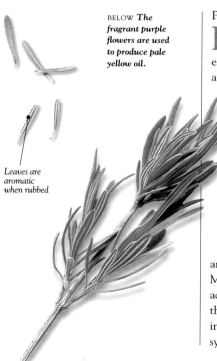

Leaves are aromatic when rubbed

PROPERTIES

Lavender is calming, soothing, antidepressant, and emotionally balancing. Its antiseptic, antibacterial, and painkilling properties make it valuable in treating cuts, wounds, and burns. Because it is also a decongestant, it is effective against colds, flu, and catarrhal conditions. Lavender lowers blood pressure, prevents and eases spasms, is antirheumatic, and also a tonic. Most importantly, lavender is an adaptogen, meaning that it has the ability to restore balance and initiate healing in any body system that is out of balance.

METHODS OF USE

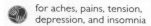 for aches, pains, tension, depression, and insomnia

 for digestive problems

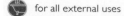 for all external uses

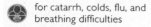 for catarrh, colds, flu, and breathing difficulties

for burns, cuts, rashes, and headaches

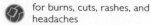 for sore throats, gums, and bad breath

Blends well with
• Florals such as rose, geranium, ylang ylang, chamomile, and jasmine
• Citrus oils such as orange, lemon, bergamot, and grapefruit
• Rosemary, marjoram, patchouli, clary sage, chamomile, cedarwood, clove, and tea tree

Suggested blends
FOR BACKACHE
4 drops lavender
3 drops eucalyptus
3 drops ginger

FOR EARACHE
2 drops lavender
2 drops tea tree
6 drops chamomile

FOR IRRITABILITY
3 drops lavender
4 drops chamomile
3 drops neroli

MAIN USES

Skin problems such as burns, bruises, spots, allergies, and insect bites benefit. Problems of the nervous system such as tension, depression, insomnia, headaches, stress, and hypertension respond particularly well. It can be used to relieve stomach cramps, nausea, colic, flatulence, and indigestion. It also helps to ease cystitis, relieve asthma, catarrhal conditions, throat infections, and helps to clear bad breath.

ABOVE *Lavender oil increases the therapeutic benefits of any oil with which it is blended.*

CAUTIONS
Usually safe for all age groups, but some hay fever or asthma sufferers may be allergic.

LAVENDER WATER
Pour ⅓ cup rosewater into a bottle and add 30 drops of lavender oil. Shake well, leave in the dark for two weeks. Use as a skin tonic.

Tea tree

MELALEUCA ALTERNIFOLIA

THIS SMALL TREE *or shrub is a traditional remedy among the aboriginal people of Australia. More recently, scientific studies have shown that tea tree oil can combat all types of infection – bacterial, fungal, and viral. It also supports the immune system in its fight against infection.*

Tea tree leaves are highly antiseptic

PROPERTIES

Primarily an anti-infection oil, tea tree has antifungal, antibacterial, and antiviral properties. It also helps to stop the spread of infection. It is an expectorant that also alleviates inflammation and stimulates the immune system. It helps to heal wounds when applied externally by encouraging the formation of scar tissue and can be used to treat dandruff. Tea tree kills parasites such as fleas and lice and also has cleansing and deodorizing properties.

ABOVE **The leaves and twigs of the shrub are used to produce the oil.**

RIGHT **Tea tree is very good for skin problems and can often be applied neat.**

METHODS OF USE

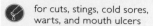 for cuts, stings, cold sores, warts, and mouth ulcers

for throat and mouth infections

for colds, flu, and respiratory infections

for vaginal and urinary tract infections

for athlete's foot, blisters

for chicken pox and shingles, blisters, rashes

for sickrooms, colds, breathing problems

for dandruff

Blends well with
- Lavender, geranium, chamomile, myrrh
- Lemon, rosemary, marjoram, clary sage, pine
- Spice oils such as nutmeg, clove, and cinnamon

Suggested blends

FOR RESPIRATORY INFECTIONS
5 drops tea tree
3 drops pine
2 drops thyme

FOR SPOTS AND ACNE
3 drops bergamot
3 drops lavender
4 drops tea tree

FOR THE MOUTH AND GUMS
5 drops tea tree
5 drops myrrh

MAIN USES

Tea tree is frequently used for skincare problems such as spots and acne, warts, oily skin, athlete's foot, rashes, insect bites, and even burns and blisters. It helps to heal cuts and infected wounds and is effective against dandruff, cold sores, and urinary or genital infections such as cystitis and thrush. It is also valuable in fighting colds, flu, respiratory infections, catarrhal problems, and infectious illnesses. It is also used to stimulate sweating to bring down a fever.

Tea tree is a common ingredient in toothpastes, shampoos, gargles, and deodorants, and in some medicated skincare soaps.

CAUTION
People with sensitive skin should introduce the oil with caution.

RIGHT *A footbath using tea tree oil is ideal for athlete's foot and for soothing aching, blistered feet.*

Rosemary
ROSMARINUS OFFICINALIS

ROSEMARY WAS ONE *of the first herbs to be used medicinally.
Traditionally, it was used to ward off evil, offer protection from
the plague, and to preserve and flavor meat. It remains a popular
culinary and medicinal herb and the oil is regarded as one of the
most valuable of all essential oils.*

Flowers can be
either light blue
or pink

Spiky silvery
green leaves

PROPERTIES

Rosemary stimulates the
circulation and acts as a
tonic for the nervous system,
skin, liver, and gall bladder. It is
refreshing, antiseptic, and
antibacterial. It is also diuretic
and generally cleansing.
Rosemary has antidepressant and
antifungal properties; it prevents
and reduces spasms, relieves
wind, and regulates digestion.
It clears catarrh and kills
pain. On an emotional
level the oil relieves
mental exhaustion
and promotes
mental clarity.

ABOVE **Rosemary is a
native Mediterranean
plant. France and Spain
are two of the main oil-
producing countries.**

LEFT **Rosemary was
once considered
the great "cure
all" of all herbs.**

METHODS OF USE

 for muscular aches and strains, fluid retention, period pain, poor circulation

 for colds, coughs, headaches, and catarrh

 for aches, sprains, headaches, and digestive problems

 as a tonic, for period pain and fluid retention

 for dandruff and hair loss

 for apathy and fatigue

Blends well with
• Frankincense, petitgrain, basil, thyme, bergamot
• Lavender, peppermint, pine, cedarwood, cypress
• Spice oils such as cinnamon, clove, ginger, black pepper

Suggested blends

FOR CONSTIPATION
4 drops rosemary
4 drops orange
2 drops black pepper

FOR MUSCLE STRAIN
3 drops rosemary
3 drops ginger
4 drops lavender

FOR FLUID RETENTION
4 drops lemon
3 drops rosemary
3 drops patchouli

MAIN USES

An excellent oil for muscle and mental fatigue, coughs and colds, poor circulation, aches, pains, and strains. It is also used for acne, eczema, dandruff, lice, and hair loss. Useful for fluid retention, painful periods, flatulence, indigestion, and constipation. Headaches, low blood pressure, and stress-related disorders also benefit.

ABOVE *The colorless or pale yellow oil has a strong herbal fragrance.*

WIDE AWAKE SHOWER GEL

If you are tired and sluggish in the mornings, mix the following oils with a little of unscented shower gel and work to a lather with a sponge.

• 1 drop rosemary
• 2 drops petitgrain
• 1 drop grapefruit

CAUTIONS
Do not use during pregnancy. Rosemary is not suitable for people with epilepsy or high blood pressure.

Clary sage

SALVIA SCLAREA

AFFECTIONATELY KNOWN *as "clear eye," clary sage was used in medieval times for clearing foreign bodies from the eyes. Although it is now less well known than common garden sage, clary remains popular in aromatherapy because it is nontoxic and has a pleasant nutty fragrance. The effects of clary sage have been described as "euphoric."*

PROPERTIES

Clary is antidepressant and sometimes described as euphoric. For many people it is simply relaxing and soothing because of its regulating effect on the nervous system. It is also used to help digestion and as a powerful muscle relaxant. Its astringent properties make it beneficial for oily skin and scalp conditions. Clary can also be used to help prevent and arrest convulsions. It is effective against bacteria and may benefit menstruation. As well as lowering blood pressure, clary is also renowned as an aphrodisiac.

Tall flower spikes are supported by yellow and purple bracts

Clary has many of the properties of sage

ABOVE *Clary sage is native to Italy, Syria, and southern France.*

METHODS OF USE

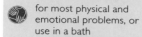

for most physical and emotional problems, or use in a bath

for stress, depression, headaches, and throat infections

for digestive disorders and period pain

for throat infections

for skin conditions

Blends well with
• Lavender, frankincense, sandalwood, cedarwood
• Citrus oils such as lemon, orange, and bergamot
• Geranium, ylang ylang, juniper, coriander

Suggested blends
FOR ANXIETY
4 drops clary sage
3 drops ylang ylang
3 drops lavender

FOR THE MENOPAUSE
5 drops clary sage
2 drops chamomile
3 drops geranium

AS AN APHRODISIAC
4 drops clary sage
4 drops sandalwood
2 drops black pepper

MAIN USES

This oil is most beneficial in treating anxiety, depression, and stress-related problems. It is useful for absent or scanty periods and PMS. It can lower blood pressure and relieve indigestion and flatulence. It helps to ease muscular aches and pains and is good for throat and respiratory infections. Clary sage can also benefit frigidity and impotence.

ABOVE *The oil is colorless with a nutty, herbaceous aroma.*

CAUTIONS

Do not use during pregnancy. Do not use when drinking alcohol as it can make you drunk, drowsy, and can cause nightmares.

RIGHT *Gargling with clary sage is a safe and effective treatment for throat infections.*

Eucalyptus

EUCALYPTUS GLOBULUS

SEVERAL OF THE 700 species of eucalyptus are used to distil medicinal quality essential oil, but the Australian "blue gum" is by far the most widely used. Eucalyptus is a traditional remedy in Australia and a familiar ingredient in numerous chest rubs and decongestants. In aromatherapy the oil has many varied uses.

ABOVE **Both old and young leaves are distilled to yield a colorless oil with a distinctive aroma.**

BELOW **Only about 15 of the hundreds of species yield a valuable oil.**

Leaves of mature trees are long, pointed, and yellowy-green

PROPERTIES

Eucalyptus is a powerful antiseptic and renowned decongestant. It also has strong antiviral properties. Eucalyptus alleviates inflammation generally, and is helpful in treating rheumatism. The oil also has insecticidal properties, and can be used to eliminate parasites. It is a diuretic and a deodorant. It stimulates the immune system and is an effective local painkiller, especially for nerve pain. Other properties include its ability to reduce fevers and heal wounds by promoting the formation of scar tissue.

METHODS OF USE

 for coughs, colds, flu, sinus problems, and chest infections

 for muscular and rheumatic pain

 to purify the air in a sickroom

 as a mosquito repellent

 for the blisters of chicken pox and shingles, and insect bites

 for cuts and wounds

Blends well with
- Peppermint, tea tree
- Rosemary, thyme, lavender
- Cedarwood, lemon, pine

Suggested blends

FOR CHILDHOOD ILLNESSES
3 drops eucalyptus
3 drops chamomile
4 drops lavender

FOR CHEST INFECTIONS
4 drops eucalyptus,
2 drops thyme
2 drops pine
1 drop lavender

WARNING
Do not take internally as ingesting even small amounts can be fatal.

MAIN USES

Used mostly for coughs, colds, chest infections, and sinusitis. It is also valuable in preventing the spread of infection. Eucalyptus soothes muscular aches and pains such as rheumatism and fibrositis. It is also beneficial in treating skin infections, cuts, and blisters, including the blisters associated with genital and oral herpes, chicken pox, and shingles. Urinary tract problems such as cystitis also respond well. When used to treat burns, eucalyptus eases the pain and helps new tissue to form. It helps to prevent and relieve insect bites and is an effective mosquito repellent.

CAUTIONS

Do not take when using homeopathic remedies. Do not use for more than a few days at a time because of risk of toxicity. Do not use on babies or very young children.

RIGHT *Eucalyptus oil is used in ointments, liniments, and cough remedies.*

Geranium

PELARGONIUM GRAVEOLENS

THE FAMILIAR POTTED GERANIUM *has a long history of use in herbal medicine. Over 700 varieties exist and their essential oils differ depending on where the plant is grown. Fresh and floral in fragrance, geranium was traditionally regarded as a feminine oil, a powerful healer and valuable insect repellent.*

BELOW **Both the fresh leaves and small pink flowers of the plant are distilled for their essential oil.**

The odor of the blossoms superficially resembles that of the rose

The fresh green leaves give the oil its green color

PROPERTIES

Geranium is mentally uplifting and refreshing. It has a balancing effect on the nervous system and is said to be a wonderful antidepressant. The anti-inflammatory, soothing, and astringent properties of geranium account for its success and popularity in skin care. Its antiseptic properties make it useful for cuts and infections. It is also thought to be deodorant, diuretic, and balancing for mind and body. It stimulates the lymphatic system, stops bleeding, and can be used as a tonic for the liver and kidneys.

METHODS OF USE

 for all emotional, circulation, hormonal, and arthritic problems

 for all problems except throat and mouth infections

 for skin complaints

 for sore throat, tonsillitis, and mouth infections

 to deodorize a room

Blends well with
• Lavender, bergamot, rose, rosewood
• Sandalwood, patchouli, frankincense, lemon, jasmine
• Juniper, tea tree, benzoin, basil, black pepper

Suggested blends
FOR HEALTHY SKIN
4 drops geranium
2 drops bergamot
3 drops rose

FOR DEPRESSION
5 drops geranium
3 drops benzoin
2 drops bergamot

FOR PMS
5 drops geranium
3 drops clary sage
2 drops rose

MAIN USES

An effective treatment for numerous skin problems such as acne, diaper rash, burns, blisters, eczema, cuts, and congested pores. Regarded as a feminine oil, geranium is also used to treat PMS and menopausal problems. Its excellent draining properties help to relieve swollen breasts and fluid retention and it stimulates sluggish lymph and blood circulation.

ABOVE *Geranium oil has a light, rose-like fragrance.*

Arthritis and neuralgia are relieved by geranium, and sore throats and mouth ulcers benefit from its antiseptic properties. Geranium is also believed to be emotionally balancing, helping to alleviate apathy, anxiety, stress, hyperactivity, and also depression.

CAUTIONS

May irritate the skin of some hypersensitive individuals. Do not use during the first three months of pregnancy and not at all if there is a history of miscarriage.

Lemon

CITRUS LIMON

LEMON IS MORE COMMONLY *regarded as a nutritious fruit rather than a healing agent, but it has a history of therapeutic use throughout Europe. The essential oil which is expressed from the fresh peel has many varied applications, making it invaluable in the home aromatherapy kit.*

PROPERTIES

The most important property of lemon is its ability to stimulate the body's defenses to fight infection. The oil is also refreshing and has a tonic effect on the circulation. It is antiseptic and a wonderful antibacterial. Lemon is astringent, diuretic, and laxative and has the ability to arrest bleeding. It may also lower blood pressure, prevent and relieve rheumatism, and reduce a fever. Because it counteracts acidity in the body, lemon can also help to maintain a healthy acid/alkaline balance.

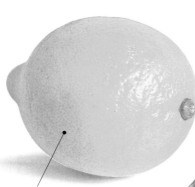

The essential oil is pressed from the outer rind of lemons

Evergreen, oval leaves

ABOVE **The lemon tree is an attractive tree of up to 20ft.(6m) with fragrant flowers, oval leaves, and bright yellow fruit.**

METHODS OF USE

 as a tonic and for most health problems

 as a room refresher or mood enhancer

 on affected skin, cuts, gums, or nosebleeds and neat on warts

 for circulation and as a tonic

 for cold and flu-like conditions

 over the site of acid indigestion or arthritic pain

Blends well with
• Lavender, rose, ylang ylang, neroli, chamomile
• Juniper, benzoin, frankincense, black pepper, basil, sandalwood
• Other citrus oils such as orange, lime, bergamot

Suggested blends
FOR CIRCULATION
6 drops lemon
3 drops cypress
4 drops ylang ylang

FOR FATIGUE
4 drops lemon
2 drops black pepper
4 drops sandalwood

FOR DEPRESSION
2 drops lemon
3 drops rose
5 drops sandalwood

MAIN USES

Lemon kills infection and stops bleeding in minor cuts and nosebleeds. It can be used to remove warts, corns, and similar growths and also helps to clear greasy skin, acne, and herpes blisters. It is beneficial in treating inflamed or diseased gums and mouth ulcers and useful for acid indigestion, arthritis, and rheumatism. It is often used to treat varicose veins, poor circulation, and high blood pressure. Lemon helps to clear colds, flu, and bronchitis. It can be used against all types of infection. Lemon dispels depression and indecision. Lemon can be used as a mild skin bleach for freckles and it also makes an effective insect repellent.

ABOVE *The greenish yellow oil has a fresh citrus fragrance.*

CAUTIONS

Can irritate sensitive skin. Do not use before sunbathing. Use only very diluted in massage and bath blends, and not for more than a few days at a time.

Peppermint
MENTHA PIPERITA

PEPPERMINT is best known as a remedy for digestive problems. It was used as such by the Romans and possibly the ancient Egyptians. Apart from its many therapeutic applications it is also used as a humane form of pest control. Peppermint grows throughout Europe but most oil comes from the United States.

ABOVE **Peppermint is a perennial herb that is grown throughout the world.**

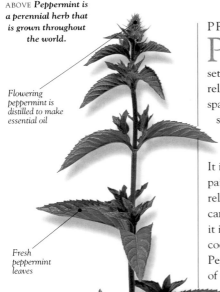

Flowering peppermint is distilled to make essential oil

Fresh peppermint leaves

PROPERTIES

Peppermint is refreshing and stimulating. It tones and settles the digestive system, relieves flatulence, and reduces spasms. It also helps to tone the stomach, liver, and intestines, while strengthening and toning the nervous system. It is a valuable expectorant, a painkiller, an antiseptic, and it relieves itching. Peppermint can reduce fevers in two ways: it induces sweating and it has a cooling effect on the body. Peppermint also promotes clarity of thought. It is often used as an emergency treatment for shock, because of its stimulant properties.

METHODS OF USE

 on a tissue for travel sickness or shock, or vaporizer in a sickroom

 for headaches and migraine

 for colds, flu, respiratory problems, headaches, sinusitis, or to steam and cleanse skin

 for sickness, diarrhea, and digestive complaints

 for colds and fevers

 footbath for chilblains

 for bad breath

Blends well with
• Lavender, chamomile, rosemary, lemon
• Eucalyptus, benzoin, sandalwood, marjoram
• Other mints such as spearmint

Suggested blends

FOR VOMITING
3 drops lavender
4 drops peppermint
3 drops chamomile

FOR HEADACHES
3 drops peppermint
4 drops lavender
3 drops rose

FOR BAD BREATH
5 drops peppermint
3 drops bergamot
2 drops myrrh

MAIN USES

Most commonly used for indigestion, diarrhea, nausea, vomiting, stomach cramps, and travel sickness. It is also used for bronchitis, colds, flu, acne, and congested skin. Beneficial for toothache, headaches, some migraines, and as an emergency remedy for shock. Muscle and mental fatigue are both relieved by peppermint and it also freshens bad breath.

ABOVE
Peppermint oil has a strong minty fragrance.

CAUTIONS

Do not use during pregnancy. May sensitize or irritate the skin in some people. Do not use while taking homeopathic remedies. Use in moderation.

PEPPERMINT INHALATION

For colds, flu, and respiratory disorders, use the oil alone or blended with other expectorant and antiseptic oils. Try:
• sandalwood and/or pine for chest infections
• eucalyptus/lavender/sandalwood for flu and catarrh

Petitgrain

CITRUS AURANTIUM

PETITGRAIN IS *often regarded as a cheaper alternative to the exquisite essential oil, neroli. Both oils come from the bitter orange tree and share similar properties and fragrances. But where neroli comes from the blossom, fresh and flowery petitgrain is distilled from the leaves and twigs.*

Petitgrain oil used to be extracted from the tiny unripe oranges

PROPERTIES

Petitgrain is a soothing oil that can be refreshing or relaxing depending on which oils it is blended with. It is a valuable antidepressant, which also strengthens and supports the nervous system and acts as a general tonic. It helps to tone the digestive system and is able to control and reduce spasms in the body, especially in the digestive system. Petitgrain is a deodorant and a gentle antiseptic. It also helps to control the overproduction of sebum in the skin and is a refreshing bath oil.

ABOVE **Citrus aurantium *is native to southern China and northeast India.***

Fresh leaves used in distillation

METHODS OF USE

 to refresh, relax, uplift, or for convalescence

 for most emotional and physical conditions

 used to cleanse greasy or spotty skin

 for depression or anxiety states

 for hair care

 for skin problems

Blends well with
• Geranium, ylang ylang, chamomile, oakmoss, jasmine
• Bergamot, lemon, orange, neroli
• Clary sage, clove, rosemary, lavender, juniper

Suggested blends

FOR ANXIETY
4 drops petitgrain
3 drops geranium
3 drops sandalwood

FOR INSOMNIA
3 drops petitgrain
4 drops lavender
3 drops ylang ylang

FOR DRY SKIN
2 drops petitgrain
5 drops chamomile
3 drops rose

RIGHT **Petitgrain can be used for the treatment of exhaustion and depression.**

MAIN USES

Ideal for many greasy skin and scalp conditions, especially acne and greasy hair. It is also sometimes used to control excessive perspiration and flatulence. Petitgrain is valuable for many stress-related problems such as nervous exhaustion and insomnia. It is helpful during convalescence or periods of exhaustion and feeling "run down." Feelings of apathy, irritability, mild depression, and anxiety can all be alleviated by refreshing petitgrain. The oil is also believed to have a comforting effect on those who feel sad and lonely.

ABOVE **The pale to deep yellow oil is a refreshing mix of floral and citrus notes.**

CAUTIONS
None known.

Ylang ylang

CANANGA ODORATA VAR. GENUINA

THE NAME OF THIS OIL *means "flower of flowers," which suits its sweet fragrance. It is distilled from the flowers of a small tree that grows in Madagascar. The large fragrant flowers can be mauve, pink, or yellow. The yellow flowers are believed to produce the best oil.*

ABOVE **Oil is extracted from the fresh flowers.**

PROPERTIES

Ylang ylang is used as a sedative and an antidepressant, and is widely regarded as a "euphoric." It is also attributed with aphrodisiac properties. On a physical level it is antiseptic and inhibits the spread of infection. It acts as a tonic for the nervous and circulatory systems, it slows a rapid heart beat and breathing, and can help lower blood pressure. It also controls the production of sebum and may be used to help balance and regulate body functions generally.

ABOVE **The fresh leaves of the tropical ylang ylang tree, which grows up to 65ft(19.8m) high.**

METHODS OF USE

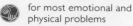

- for most emotional and physical problems
- for relaxation, and most emotional and physical problems
- for skin and hair care
- for shock and other emotional states, inhaled from a tissue

Blends well with

- Lavender, jasmine, sandalwood, chamomile, bergamot, rose, rosewood
- Patchouli, frankincense
- Citrus oils such as lemon and bergamot

Suggested blends

FOR STRESS
4 drops lavender
3 drops ylang ylang
3 drops clary sage

FOR HIGH BLOOD PRESSURE
2 drops ylang ylang
5 drops chamomile
3 drops lavender

FOR OILY SKIN
3 drops ylang ylang
3 drops lemon
4 drops geranium

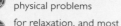

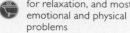

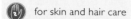

RIGHT ***The lingering sweet fragrance of ylang ylang combined with its reputation as an aphrodisiac makes it a popular ingredient in perfumes.***

MAIN USES

Ylang ylang is good for skin complaints, especially oily or irritated skin and acne, as well as bites and stings. Ylang ylang was an ingredient in the Victorian hair preparation, macassar oil, and can still be used as a scalp tonic to promote hair growth and balance sebum production in both dry and greasy scalps. Good for reducing blood pressure and for slowing breathing and heart rate in cases of shock, panic, or rage. Depression, anxiety, tension, and stress-related insomnia can also be alleviated by ylang ylang. The oil can also be used to treat sexual problems.

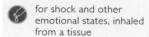

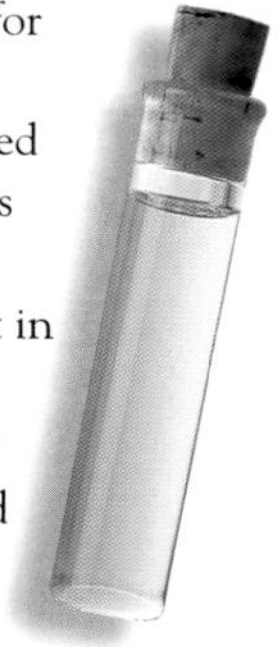

ABOVE ***Citrus oils help to tone down the intense fragrance of this pale yellow oil.***

CAUTIONS

Can cause nausea or headaches in high concentrations. May irritate some hypersensitive people. Remember to keep all essential oils out of children's reach.

Roman chamomile

CHAMAEMELUM NOBILE

CHAMOMILE IS ONE *of the most gentle of all essential oils, which makes it particularly suitable for children. There are many varieties of chamomile, but two of the most commonly used in aromatherapy are Roman chamomile and German chamomile. Both varieties share many properties and uses. Types of chamomile vary from country to country.*

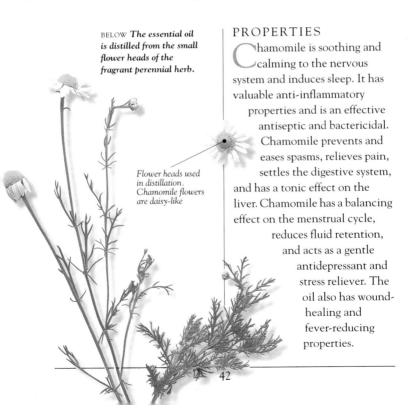

BELOW **The essential oil is distilled from the small flower heads of the fragrant perennial herb.**

Flower heads used in distillation. Chamomile flowers are daisy-like

PROPERTIES

Chamomile is soothing and calming to the nervous system and induces sleep. It has valuable anti-inflammatory properties and is an effective antiseptic and bactericidal. Chamomile prevents and eases spasms, relieves pain, settles the digestive system, and has a tonic effect on the liver. Chamomile has a balancing effect on the menstrual cycle, reduces fluid retention, and acts as a gentle antidepressant and stress reliever. The oil also has wound-healing and fever-reducing properties.

METHODS OF USE

 for tired or fretful babies, toddlers, stressed adults

 for pain, cystitis, boils, abscesses, or infected wounds

 for skin and eye problems

 for muscular pain, menstrual problems, insomnia, and stress

Blends well with
• Lavender, ylang ylang, clary sage
• Bergamot, rose, neroli, geranium
• Patchouli, lemon, basil, sandalwood, rosemary

Suggested blends
FOR BROKEN VEINS
4 drops chamomile
2 drops lemon
4 drops rose

FOR LOSS OF APPETITE
4 drops chamomile
4 drops bergamot
3 drops myrrh

FOR EARACHE
5 drops chamomile
2 drops basil
3 drops rose

MAIN USES

Calms distressed or colicky babies and relieves teething pain and earache. Also an important oil for treating insomnia, anxiety, and stress. Beneficial for digestive upsets such as indigestion, nausea, and flatulence. Many types of dull, aching pain such as headaches, toothache, menstrual pain, muscular aches and pains, arthritis, rheumatism, and neuralgia respond well to chamomile. It is a gentle but effective treatment for cuts and burns and all manner of skin problems, including skin rashes, inflammation, boils, spots, allergies, insect bites, and chilblains. Chamomile is also used to treat eye problems such as eyestrain and conjunctivitis.

CAUTIONS

Do not use in the first three months of pregnancy. Can cause dermatitis in some people. No known risk of toxicity.

LEFT *Chamomile yields a pale blue liquid which turns yellow on keeping.*

Frankincense

BOSWELLIA CARTERI

FRANKINCENSE IS *a wonderfully calming and fragrant oil. Throughout history it has been used for religious and medicinal purposes. It is still regarded as a deeply spiritual oil, but is also beneficial for treating many physical and emotional problems. Frankincense is sometimes known as olibanum.*

ABOVE **The tree is lavishly colored with small leaves and pale pink or white flowers.**

BELOW AND RIGHT **The spicy greenish or pale yellow oil is extracted from the resin of a small tree that grows in north African and some Arab countries.**

Gum resin is a natural product of the tree

PROPERTIES

Slows and deepens the breathing, relaxes mind and body. It is antiseptic, astringent, anti-inflammatory, an immune stimulant, and it encourages wound healing. Frankincense is also an expectorant and a nerve and uterine tonic. It benefits menstruation and digestion.

METHODS OF USE

 for cystitis and most urinary problems

 for most physical and emotional problems

 for meditation, anxiety, breathing difficulties

 for colds, flu, and respiratory infections

 for skin problems

 for cuts, scars, and blemishes

Blends well with
• Geranium, lavender, sandalwood, pine, cedarwood, rose, neroli, bergamot
• Spices such as cinnamon and black pepper
• Citrus oils such as orange and lemon

Suggested blends
FOR PANIC ATTACKS
4 drops lavender
4 drops frankincense
2 drops marjoram

FOR MEDITATION
6 drops frankincense
2 drops ylang ylang
2 drops bergamot

FOR AGING SKIN
3 drops frankincense
4 drops rose
3 drops clary sage

RIGHT *Frankincense oil has a fresh, slightly camphorous scent.*

MAIN USES

Frankincense is helpful in treating many respiratory and catarrhal conditions such as asthma, colds, chest infections, and chronic bronchitis. It also has many uses in skin care including the treatment of cuts, scars and blemishes, and

ABOVE *Using a vaporizer is the ideal way to benefit from frankincense's calming, expectorant, and meditative properties.*

inflammation. It is recommended for easing wrinkles and for giving tone to slack or aging skin. As a nerve tonic it benefits anxiety, depression, and nervous tension among other stress-related problems. Cystitis, hemorrhoids, irregular or heavy periods, and nosebleeds also benefit from the healing properties of frankincense.

CAUTIONS

Frankincense is safe to use during pregnancy and there are no known risks associated with its external use. As with all essential oils, keep out of children's reach and never take internally.

Rose

ROSA DAMASCENA, ROSA CENTIFOLIA

ABOVE *The essential oil is distilled from the fresh rose petals.*

TWO TYPES OF ROSE, *Damask and Cabbage, are used to produce most of the rose oil used in aromatherapy. They are slightly different in color and fragrance but have similar properties and uses. Rose oil is expensive but you need only use a little to benefit from its many therapeutic properties.*

Many rose bushes are necessary to yield a small amount of oil.

ABOVE *The traditionally "feminine" rose produces an oil particularly beneficial for women.*

PROPERTIES

Rose oil has an amazingly complex chemistry and its benefits are many and varied. It is a renowned aphrodisiac, a sedative, and a tonic with notable antidepressant properties. It is an antiseptic, powerful against both viruses and bacteria. Rose oil astringes and tones the blood and acts as a tonic for the heart, liver, stomach, and uterus.

Traditionally regarded as a feminine oil, it has a remarkable affinity with the female reproductive system. It helps to regulate the menstrual cycle and associated emotional problems. Rose also regulates the stomach and especially the appetite. It prevents and relieves spasms in the digestive system and also acts as a laxative. It is toning and soothing to the skin, stops bleeding, and brings about wound healing by encouraging the formation of scar tissue. Additionally, it helps to detoxify the blood and organs.

METHODS OF USE

 for most emotional and physical problems

 for most emotional and physical problems, especially sexual or reproductive system problems

 for emotional problems

 for headaches, conjunctivitis, nausea, and stomach problems

 for all skin conditions

Blends well with
• Most oils, especially clary sage, sandalwood, geranium, bergamot, patchouli, ylang ylang

Suggested blends

FOR HAY FEVER
3 drops rose
2 drops tea tree
5 drops lavender

FOR CHAPPED SKIN
4 drops rose
3 drops chamomile
3 drops sandalwood

FOR GRIEF
4 drops rose
2 drops frankincense
4 drops chamomile

MAIN USES

Soothes and heals cracked, chapped, sensitive, dry, inflamed, or allergy-prone skin. Broken veins, aging or wrinkled skin also benefit. It is used to improve circulation, alleviate constipation and nausea, and treat stomach problems such as peptic ulcer. Rose lifts depression, especially PMS or post-natal depression, and benefits stress-related conditions such as insomnia and nervous tension. It is also useful in treating headaches, earache, and conjunctivitis. It is an important choice for irregular or painful periods and is believed to aid conception. Hay fever, asthma, and coughs are also soothed by the scent of rose.

CAUTIONS

Do not use during the first three months of pregnancy and not at all if there is a history of miscarriage.

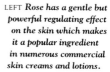

LEFT *Rose has a gentle but powerful regulating effect on the skin which makes it a popular ingredient in numerous commercial skin creams and lotions.*

Patchouli

POGOSTEMON CABLIN

THE DISTINCTIVE *earthy aroma of patchouli is one that you either love or hate. Since smell is so important to the success of aromatherapy, only use the oil if you like its fragrance. For those who do, the oil has many valuable uses and is especially pleasant when used as part of a blend.*

ABOVE **The soft green leaves of the bushy plant are fermented and dried before the essential oil is extracted by steam distillation.**

RIGHT **Patchouli is a member of the same family as basil and sage.**

Patchouli leaves are soft and furry

PROPERTIES

Astringent, antiviral, antiseptic and anti-inflammatory. In sickness it brings down fevers, prevents the spread of infection and disease, and reduces the incidence of vomiting. Patchouli soothes and settles the digestive system and acts as a tonic for the nervous system and the body generally. It counteracts the effects of poison and acts as a diuretic. Patchouli has fungicidal and deodorant actions, it is a cell regenerator, and it promotes wound healing. It is also an important antidepressant and is reputed to be an aphrodisiac.

METHODS OF USE

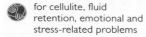 for cellulite, fluid retention, emotional and stress-related problems

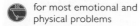 for most emotional and physical problems

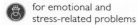 for emotional and stress-related problems

 for skin care

 dab on affected spots

 for hair care

Blends well with
• Rose, geranium, bergamot, neroli, ylang ylang, lemon
• Sandalwood, clary sage, clove, cedarwood, lavender

Suggested blends
FOR WRINKLES
2 drops patchouli
3 drops lemon
5 drops rose
FOR WOUNDS
3 drops patchouli
4 drops lavender
3 drops tea tree
FOR MOODINESS
2 drops patchouli
3 drops lemon
5 drops geranium

RIGHT *As well as imparting fragrance, the oil is believed to help prevent the spread of disease.*

MAIN USES

Among its many uses patchouli is valued in the treatment of depression, anxiety, nervous exhaustion, lack of interest in sex, and stress-related problems. Minor skin conditions such as chapped or cracked skin and open pores also respond well and it is effective in treating more serious skin problems such as acne, eczema, and dermatitis. Patchouli is one of the few oils recommended for cellulite. It is used with some success in the treatment of fluid retention and is one of the best choices for fungal infections on the skin. Hair and scalp problems such as dandruff and greasy hair can also benefit.

ABOVE *The essential oil is earthy in appearance and fragrance. Dark amber in color with a strong musty-sweet aroma, it is widely used in food and drink production to mask unpleasant tastes and smells.*

CAUTIONS
None known.

Sandalwood

SANTALUM ALBUM

THE SWEET *woody oriental smell of sandalwood is one of the most appealing fragrances of all essential oils, which explains its traditional use as a perfume and incense. The best sandalwood oil comes from India where it has been used for at least 4,000 years for medicinal and religious purposes.*

ABOVE **The oil is extracted by steam distillation mainly from the heartwood of mature sandalwood trees which grow in India. Only trees over 30 years old are suitable for essential oil production.**

PROPERTIES

Sandalwood is an antiseptic, especially effective for the urinary system. It is also bactericidal and astringent and a trusted insect repellent. It relieves fluid retention, clears catarrh, and encourages wound healing. Although it is a sedative, it also acts as a general tonic for the body. The oil contains constituents that soothe the stomach, reduce spasms, especially in the digestive system, and reduce inflammation. Sandalwood is antidepressant and generally calming to the nervous system. Its aphrodisiac properties are widely acclaimed.

ABOVE **Dry sandalwood chippings impregnated with the sweet woody fragrance can be used as incense.**

METHODS OF USE

 for skin conditions

 for relaxation and most health problems

 apply to sores or patches of affected skin and to the chest for respiratory conditions

 for respiratory problems

 for throats (although it tastes bitter)

 for relaxation, as an aphrodisiac

Blends well with
• Lavender, rose, ylang ylang, geranium, chamomile
• Patchouli, bergamot, frankincense, black pepper, benzoin
• Tea tree, juniper, myrrh, cypress

Suggested blends

FOR HORMONAL BALANCE
3 drops sandalwood
4 drops clary sage
3 drops lavender

FOR SUNBURN
3 drops sandalwood
3 drops lavender
4 drops chamomile

TO STRENGTHEN THE
IMMUNE SYSTEM
4 drops sandalwood
2 drops tea tree
4 drops lavender

MAIN USES

Sandalwood has always been used to treat respiratory conditions and is still effective for bronchitis, dry coughs, and sore throats. It has also proved itself an effective antiseptic for all urinary disorders, especially disorders of the urinary tract such as cystitis. Skin problems such as dry chapped skin, acne, psoriasis, eczema, and shaving rash can also benefit from its soothing, rehydrating, and antiseptic action. The fragrance can also help to lift depression and banish feelings of anxiety and sexual disinterest.

CAUTIONS
None known.

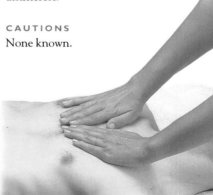

BELOW *As a reputed aphrodisiac, sandalwood is an essential ingredient in a sensual massage blend.*

Home use

ESSENTIAL OILS *make a pleasant alternative to the usual items in the home or travel first aid kit. For such basic care you need invest in only six or seven multi-purpose oils. Keep a ready supply of base oil, cotton wool, cotton cloth, sticking plasters, and bandages. Aromatherapy oils should always be kept out of reach of children, but they can be used successfully for many accidents and childhood ailments.*

ESSENTIAL ITEMS FOR THE HOME

- tea tree
- lavender
- chamomile
- lemon
- eucalyptus
- peppermint
- rosemary
- vegetable oil for blending
- cotton wool/tissues
- mixing bottle
- cotton for compresses
- bandages/plasters
- vaporizer

PLAY SAFE

Do not expect to use essential oils to deal with conditions that would normally require medical attention. In all cases of serious shock, wounds, or injuries call a physician and stay with the patient until he or she arrives.

ABOVE *Applying an aromatherapy oil before doing stretching exercises can help you relax.*

BELOW *This basic first aid kit is ideal for most everyday problems.*

Cotton compress

Cotton wool

Mixing bottle

Rosemary   Lavender   Tea tree   Chamomile   Blending oil   Lemon   Peppermint

Common ailments

HERE ARE *a few of the common health problems that you should be able to treat at home with considerable success. Remember: if symptoms persist or deteriorate, consult a professional aromatherapist or see your physician.*

ALLERGIES 🍃

Choose calming oils such as lavender (*pp.22–3*) and chamomile (*pp.42–3*). Also rose (*pp.46–7*), sandalwood (*pp.50–51*), and ylang ylang (*pp.40–41*). Use in massage, baths, compresses, inhalations, and lotions depending on the nature of the allergy.

ANEMIA 🍃

Lemon (*pp.34–5*), thyme, and chamomile (*pp.42–3*) in massage oil and in a bath.

ARTHRITIS 🍃

Painkilling oils such as chamomile (*pp.42–3*), lavender (*pp.22–3*), and rosemary (*pp.26–7*) in a bath, in local massage, and as a compress on affected area. Black pepper, ginger, and marjoram improve circulation.

ATHLETE'S FOOT 🍃

A foot bath with tea tree oil (*pp.24–5*), eucalyptus (*pp.30–31*), patchouli (*pp.48–9*), myrrh, and/or lavender (*pp.22–3*) is effective as all the oils are soothing and antifungal. Also add to unscented skin lotion.

CELLULITE 🍃

A blend of geranium (*pp.32–3*) and rosemary (*pp.26–7*) or grapefruit, juniper or cypress used in massage and skin lotion, or add to a bath and use a loofah to stimulate the tissues.

CHILBLAINS

Lemon (*pp.34–5*), lavender (*pp.22–3*), chamomile (*pp.42–3*), cypress, peppermint (*pp.36–7*), or black pepper in massage, in a bath or footbath, or dabbed on the affected area.

COLD SORES

Eucalyptus (*pp.30–31*), bergamot, lemon (*pp.34–5*), or tea tree (*pp.24–5*) are effective. Dab on tea tree (*pp.24–5*) neat or mixed with vodka before the blisters come out. Alternate its use with lavender (*pp.22–3*) to soothe.

COLDS

Lavender (*pp.22–3*), eucalyptus (*pp.30–31*), and tea tree (*pp.24–5*), or rosemary (*pp.26–7*) and peppermint (*pp.36–7*), used in a bath or steam inhalation. A bath using lavender (*pp.22–3*) and marjoram helps reduce aches and feverishness.

COUGHS

Steam inhalation using tea tree (*pp.24–5*), thyme, eucalyptus (*pp.30–31*), lavender (*pp.22–3*), or frankincense (*pp.44–5*). Sandalwood (*pp.50–51*) is good for dry coughs. It also works well massaged into the chest and throat.

CYSTITIS

Chamomile (*pp.42–3*), sandalwood (*pp.50–51*), lavender (*pp.22–3*), frankincense (*pp.44–5*), or tea tree (*pp.24–5*) in baths and washes at least once a day. Use a weak dilution; about 1 percent in boiled and cooled water as a compress.

DANDRUFF

Rosemary (*pp.26–7*), cedarwood, tea tree (*pp.24–5*), or patchouli (*pp.48–9*) massaged into the scalp, added to unscented shampoos, and used in the final rinse when you are washing your hair.

DEPRESSION

For depression with sleeplessness use lavender (*pp.22–3*), sandalwood (*pp.50–51*), chamomile (*pp.42–3*), clary sage (*pp.28–9*), or ylang ylang (*pp.40–41*). With lethargy use bergamot, geranium (*pp.32–3*), rose (*pp.46–7*). With anxiety try ylang ylang (*pp.40–41*) and neroli. Massage

is best, where possible. therwise use
the oils in the bath or in a vaporizer.

DIARRHEA 🍃

Chamomile (pp.42–3), lavender
(pp.22–3), and/or peppermint
(pp.36–7) added to a bath or
massaged over the abdomen.
Eucalyptus (pp.30–31)
is helpful if the
diarrhea is caused by a
viral infection.

ECZEMA 🍃

Lavender (pp.22–3), chamomile
(pp.42–3), sandalwood
(pp.50–51), rose (pp.46–7),
melissa, or geranium
(pp.32–3) in a bath and
massage. Add the oils to
unscented skin lotion or
aqueous cream and rub into
the skin. A cool compress
can help to soothe
irritated patches.

FAINTING 🍃

Put a couple of drops of
peppermint (pp.36–7),
lavender (pp.22–3), or rosemary
(pp.26–7) on a tissue to inhale or
hold an open bottle containing one
of these essential oils under the
person's nose.

GINGIVITIS 🍃

(Inflammation of the gums)
Mouthwashes made with
tea tree (pp.24–5) or thyme
can kill the bacteria that
cause infection. Add myrrh
for healing and orange to
strengthen the gums.

GLANDULAR FEVER 🍃

Tea tree oil (pp.24–5) is antiviral and
strengthens the immune system. Use
in a bath and in massage.

HAIR LOSS
AND BALDNESS 🍃

Lavender (pp.22–3), rosemary
(pp.26–7), sage,
cedarwood, patchouli
(pp.48–9), or ylang ylang
(pp.40–41) massaged
into the scalp and added to
mild unfragranced shampoos.

HANGOVER 🍃

Lavender (pp.22–3),
grapefruit, rosemary
(pp.26–7), juniper, fennel,
or sandalwood (pp.50–51)
in a bath, in unscented shower gel as
an inhalation, or in a vaporizer.

HAY FEVER 🍃

Chamomile (pp.42–3) in the bath and
in massage. Steam or dry inhalations

of lavender (*pp.22–3*) and/or eucalyptus (*pp.30–31*) for sneezing and runny nose. Also use in a bath.

HEADACHES ❧

Neat lavender (*pp.22–3*) rubbed into the temples, forehead, or back of the neck. Add peppermint (*pp.36–7*) if you want to stay alert. Inhalations of lavender (*pp.22–3*), peppermint (*pp.36–7*), or eucalyptus (*pp.30–31*).

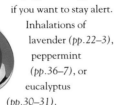

HEMORRHOIDS ❧

Frankincense (*pp.44–5*), geranium (*pp.32–3*), or juniper used in a bath, in a skin lotion, or on a cool compress. If constipation is part of the problem, massage the abdomen with rosemary (*pp.26–7*).

INDIGESTION ❧

Gently massage chamomile (*pp.42–3*), lavender (*pp.22–3*), peppermint (*pp.36–7*), rosemary (*pp.26–7*), or clary sage (*pp.28–9*) over the stomach or apply as a hot compress.

INFLUENZA ❧

Add eucalyptus (*pp.30–31*), lavender (*pp.22–3*), peppermint (*pp.36–7*), or

tea tree (*pp.24–5*) to a hot bath at the first sign of illness. Also use in steam inhalation.

INSOMNIA ❧

Lavender (*pp.22–3*) and chamomile (*pp.42–3*), sandalwood (*pp.50–51*), rose (*pp.46–7*) and/or ylang ylang (*pp.40–41*). Use in a warm bath at bedtime, in massage, or in a vaporizer. Try 2 drops of lavender (*pp.22–3*) on a tissue tucked under your pillow.

ME 🌿

Tea tree (*pp.24–5*) strengthens the immune system, rosemary (*pp.26–7*) has a tonic effect, geranium (*pp.32–3*) is an antidepressant. Massage is best where possible, but baths and vaporizers are also useful.

NAUSEA AND VOMITING 🌿

Relieve with lavender
chamomile
, peppermint
), rose (*pp.46–7*), or
ood (*pp.50–51*)
on a warm
ss laid over the
h. Gently
ge over the
ch area. Use
aporizer.

URALGIA 🌿

: lavender (*pp.22–3*),
imomile (*pp.42–3*),
–7*), geranium
(*pp.32–3*), clary sage (*pp.28–9*), or eucalyptus (*pp.30–31*) in the bath or most effectively on a hot compress applied to the affected area.

PERIOD PROBLEMS 🌿

• Heavy: geranium (*pp.32–3*), chamomile (*pp.42–3*), frankincense (*pp.44–5*), rose (*pp.46–7*).

• Irregular: clary sage (*pp.28–9*), chamomile (*pp.42–3*), lavender (*pp.22–3*), peppermint (*pp.36–7*), rose (*pp.46–7*).

• Scanty: lavender (*pp.22–3*), peppermint (*pp.36–7*), rose (*pp.46–7*).

• Painful: clary sage (*pp.28–9*), geranium (*pp.32–3*), lavender (*pp.22–3*), chamomile (*pp.42–3*), rose (*pp.46–7*). Use in a bath, in massage, and as a compress.

PMS 🌿

Clary sage (*pp.28–9*), lavender (*pp.22–3*), and chamomile (*pp.42–3*). Use rosemary (*pp.26–7*) and geranium (*pp.32–3*) for fluid retention and bloating. For irritability and depression choose rose (*pp.46–7*) and chamomile (*pp.42–3*). Use in massage, a bath, and a vaporizer.

PSORIASIS

Sedative and antidepressant oils such as lavender (*pp.22–3*) and chamomile (*pp.42–3*) can help to reduce the stress that exacerbates the condition. Use in a bath, massage, and skin creams.

STRESS

Use any of the sedative oils to help you relax, e.g., lavender (*pp.22–3*), chamomile (*pp.42–3*), rose (*pp.46–7*), clary sage (*pp.28–9*) in a bath or in massage. For short periods of stress try rosemary (*pp.26–7*), geranium (*pp.32–3*), or peppermint (*pp.36–7*).

THRUSH

Baths, massage, and local applications of antifungal oils such as lavender (*pp.22–3*), tea tree (*pp.24–5*), myrrh, geranium (*pp.32–3*), and bergamot for vaginal thrush. Use a mouthwash made with myrrh for oral thrush.

VARICOSE VEINS

Cypress, lemon (*pp.34–5*), rosemary (*pp.26–7*), lavender (*pp.22–3*), or juniper used in a bath or compress. They can be mixed with a skin cream and rubbed gently over the area. If using massage, work gently below the affected area, never above. Vary your choice of oils.

Further reading

THE ILLUSTRATED ENCYCLOPEDIA OF ESSENTIAL OILS by *Julia Lawless* (Element)

AROMATHERAPY AN A–Z by *Patricia Davis* (CW Daniel)

PRACTICAL AROMATHERAPY by *Shirley Price* (Thorsons)

THE FRAGRANT PHARMACY by *Valerie Ann Worwood* (Bantam)

THE FRAGRANT MIND by *Valerie Ann Worwood* (Doubleday)

AROMATHERAPY BLENDS AND REMEDIES by *Franzesca Watson* (Thorsons)

PRINCIPLES OF AROMATHERAPY by *Cathy Hopkins* (Thorsons)

HEALTH ESSENTIALS: AROMATHERAPY by *Christine Wildwood* (Element)

Useful addresses

FOR INFORMATION
Aromatherapy Organizations Council
3 Latymer Close, Braybrooke
Market Harborough
Leicester LE16 8LN
Tel: 01858 434242

Aromatherapy Trade Council
PO Box 52, Market Harborough
Leicester LE16 8ZX
Tel: 01858 465731

American Alliance of Aromatherapy
PO Box 750428, Petaluma,
CA 94975–0428 USA
Tel: 1 707 778 6762
Fax: 1 707 769 0868

American Aromatherapy Association
PO Box 3679, South Pasadena
CA 91031 USA
Tel: 1 818 457 1742

National Association of Holistic Aromatherapy
PO Box 17622, Boulder
CO 80308–0622 USA
Tel: 1 303 258 3791

TO FIND A PRACTITIONER
International Federation of Aromatherapists
Stamford House
2–4 Chiswick High Road
London W4 1TH
Tel: 0181 742 2602
(Send an A5 s.a.e. and a cheque for £2 for a list of practitioners)